Trip to Santa Fe with

Kayla
Fiona
Donna
&
me

Picking up Fiona to take her
to Minnesota for summer

Appetizers & Beverages from

Santa Fe KITCHENS

Among the Aspens, 1939, by E. Martin Hennings, oil on canvas. Collection of the New Mexico Museum of Art, contributed in loving memory of Simon and Maud Herzstein by Isobel Herzstein Lord, 2006. Photo by Blair Clark.

Appetizers & Beverages from

Santa Fe KITCHENS

THE MUSEUM OF NEW MEXICO FOUNDATION

MEMBERS AND FRIENDS

Gibbs Smith, Publisher

TO ENRICH AND INSPIRE HUMANKIND

Salt Lake City | Charleston | Santa Fe | Santa Barbara

First Edition
12 11 10 09 08   5 4 3 2 1

Published by
Gibbs Smith, Publisher
P.O. Box 667
Layton, Utah 84041

Orders: 1.800.835.4993
www.gibbs-smith.com

Designed by TTA Design
Printed and bound in China

Library of Congress Cataloging-in-Publication Data
Appetizers and beverages from Santa Fe kitchens / The Museum of
New Mexico Foundation. – 1st ed.
      p. cm.
  Includes index.
  ISBN-13: 978-1-4236-0338-2
  ISBN-10: 1-4236-0338-9
  1. Appetizers. 2. Beverages. I. Museum of New Mexico
Foundation.
  TX740.A6998 2008
  641.8'12—dc22
                              2007028174

Contents

Preface

For centuries, Santa Fe has charmed visitors. A central ingredient in the making of Santa Fe's charm has been the kitchens of the city and the surrounding area. Whether in the home or in restaurants, Santa Fe kitchens reflect the diversity of the city and its residents and visitors. Blending the diverse cultures of New Mexico, Native American, Hispanic, Anglo and others, Santa Fe kitchens daily create a unique and compelling cuisine that is both local and worldly in its tastes and appeal.

The Museum of New Mexico Foundation, a private nonprofit organization, is dedicated to the support of four state museums in Santa Fe – the Palace of the Governors, the New Mexico Museum of Arts, the Museum of International Folk Art and the Museum of Indian Arts & Culture – and six historical state monuments that comprise the Museum of New Mexico. To help create our initial cookbook, *Santa Fe Kitchens,* the Museum of New Mexico Foundation sought recipes from its membership, local chefs, artists and dignitaries. Out of more than 1,000 recipes submitted for consideration, the experts on the Museum of New Mexico Foundation's Cookbook Committee selected over 200 for this, our second cookbook. The recipes in the cookbook reflect the balance of Santa Fe's cultures and lifestyle; the simple and the complex,

artistic and basic, fun yet challenging, and, of course, spicy, with some of the most refreshing beverages you will ever see in a cookbook. Where else could you enjoy both Sesame Shrimp Toasts with Chile Pesto and Southwest Tomatillo Duck Triangles and wash them down with Santa Fe Lemonade but from a unique cookbook that reflects Santa Fe kitchens.

No book produced by the Museum of New Mexico Foundation on Santa Fe Kitchens would be complete without a discussion of the wonderful cultural institutions the foundation supports. Throughout the book we show works from the collections of the Museums of New Mexico, primarily featuring artwork from our Museum of Indian Arts & Culture. Having celebrated its twentieth anniversary in 2007, the Museum of Indian Arts & Culture is one of the world's most important museums devoted to Native art, and especially to the Native Americans of the Southwest. Dr. Shelby J. Tisdale, Ph.D., Director of the Museum of Indian Arts & Culture and the Laboratory of Anthropology, has written the following introduction, which relates the history and mission of this wonderful museum.

– Cookbook Committee

In 2007, the Museum of Indian Arts & Culture in Santa Fe, New Mexico, celebrates its twentieth anniversary as one of the world's premier institutions dedicated to the accurate and sensitive interpretation of the complex and diverse Native peoples of the Southwest. It is here, among the masterworks of Native American artistic achievement, that one can listen to Native voices as they describe their origins and histories through rich stories and songs. While learning about the history of the region's Indian cultures, visitors also witness examples of their most recent artistic expressions in pottery, textiles, basketry, and jewelry.

The Museum of Indian Arts & Culture grew out of the need for the Laboratory of Anthropology to provide a place where its collections could be viewed by the public. Together, the museum and the laboratory realize the dreams of early cultural leaders who encouraged the sensitive collection and preservation of Native American arts and material culture. Today the Museum of Indian Arts & Culture introduces the world to the Native peoples of the Southwest by providing a public space for exhibitions, artist demonstrations, and educational programs, while the Laboratory of Anthropology is a leader in archaeological and historical research. Both are renowned for their pioneering approach to the interpretation of Native arts and cultures; collaborating closely with Native communities to achieve public appreciation for their historic and living traditions.

Built upon a foundation of nearly a century of research, the Museum and Laboratory collections are unparalleled, with holdings of more than 10 million archaeological collections dating back to 9500 B.C. and over 80,000 ethnographic and fine art pieces dating from the 1700s to today. The collections are representative of the Pueblo, Navajo, Apache, and other indigenous cultures in the Southwest. Some of the unique works in the collection include one of the first black-on-black pots fired by the famous potter Maria Martinez of San Ildefonso Pueblo; a horse bridle that belonged to the famous Apache leader Cochise; Dorothy Dunn's personal collection of paintings made by her students at the Santa Fe Indian School; an extensive collection of Mimbres and Ancestral Puebloan ceramics; a ceremonial turquoise and shell bead cache from Chaco Canyon; and an extraordinary 151-foot-long hunting net made of human hair created around A.D. 1200.

From its inception, the Museum of Indian Arts & Culture has set out to be a different type of museum from those that normally exhibit Indian art and cultural materials. Instead of focusing on the usual anthropological or historical view of Native peoples, the Museum took a very proactive approach in presenting the Indian point of view. In 1997, the Museum completed a major renovation and added a new wing that now houses the exhibition Here, Now and Always. With over 1,300 objects from the collections, this exhibit combines the voices of living Native Americans with ancient and contemporary artifacts and interactive multimedia to tell their stories. Over 260 examples of pueblo pottery dating from A.D. 600 to the present can be found in the Buchsbaum Gallery of Southwestern Pottery. An education facility with a hands-on classroom and Children's Discovery Center were added in 2001. The Lloyd Kiva New Contemporary Indian Art Gallery features temporary exhibitions of well-known artists as well as emerging young Indian artists. In 2003, the addition of the Arnold and Doris Roland Sculpture Garden provided a space to exhibit large-scale bronze and stone sculptural works by such famous artists as Allan Houser, Tammy Garcia, Doug Hyde, and many others.

Shelby J. Tisdale, Ph.D.
Director, Museum of Indian Arts & Culture/
Laboratory of Anthropology

tigers

Antipasto

Antelope Hunt, 1938, by Narcisco Abeyta, Navajo, #54006/13. Museum of Indian Arts and Culture/Laboratory of Anthropology, Department of Cultural Affairs, www.miaclab.org. Photo by Blair Clark.

Artichoke Hors d'oeuvre

Makes 6 to 8 servings

1 can artichoke hearts, drained and
    finely chopped
1 cup grated Cheddar, Parmesan or
    Romano cheese
1/2 cup diced tomatoes

3/4 cup mayonnaise
1/2 teaspoon fresh dill
1 package dry Good Seasons Italian
    salad dressing mix, optional
1 French baguette, cut into thin slices

Preheat the broiler. Mix together all ingredients except the baguette slices. Top each slice with some artichoke mixture and place on a baking sheet. Broil until toppings are bubbly and golden brown. Serve immediately.

Note: Instead of serving on a baguette, the mixture can be baked at 350 degrees F for 20 minutes and then served on Melba toast or crackers.

Artichoke Crescent Roll

Makes 4 to 6 servings

1 small jar marinated artichoke hearts,
    drained and minced
1 cup fresh Parmesan cheese, grated

4 cloves garlic, pressed
1/4 cup mayonnaise to moisten
1 can crescent rolls, flattened

Preheat oven to 375 degrees F. In a bowl, mix artichokes, cheese, garlic and mayonnaise. Spread mixture on flattened rolls, and then roll up and bake for 15 minutes, or until golden.

Artichoke Squares

Makes 4 to 6 servings

2 (6-ounce) jars marinated artichokes
1 small onion, chopped
1 clove garlic, minced
4 eggs
1/4 cup breadcrumbs

1/4 teaspoon pepper
1/4 teaspoon oregano
1/4 teaspoon Tabasco Sauce
3 tablespoons chopped fresh parsley
8 ounces Cheddar cheese, grated

Preheat oven to 350 degrees F. Drain the oil from 1 jar of artichokes into a skillet. Discard the oil from the other jar. Chop the artichokes and set aside. Sauté onions and garlic in the oil until tender. Beat the eggs in a medium bowl until frothy. Add the breadcrumbs and the seasonings. Stir in the cheese, artichokes and sautéed onions. Put the mixture into a buttered 11 x 7-inch glass dish and bake for 35 to 45 minutes, or until top is golden brown. Cut into small squares and serve warm or at room temperature.

Tomato Tarts

Makes 2 tarts, serves 12 to 16

1 package pie crusts, 2 (9 inch)
Dijon mustard
1/2 pound grated Gruyère cheese
1/2 pound Asiago cheese
Coarsely ground pepper

6 to 7 large tomatoes, sliced 1/4 inch thick
Freshly chopped basil leaves

Preheat oven to 375 degrees F. Cut rounded edges off pie crusts so you have rectangles. Brush a light coating of Dijon mustard on each pastry rectangle. Mix the two cheeses together in a bowl and spread evenly over each rectangle. Sprinkle with pepper, and then cover with tomato slices, trimming to fit so they are tightly layered. Fold edges of pastry to form 1/2-inch border. Bake until crust is brown, about 40 to 45 minutes. Sprinkle with basil and cut into slices; serve warm.

Oregano-Flavored Feta Spread

Makes about 1 cup

1-1/4 cups crumbled feta cheese, separated
4 ounces cream cheese

1 teaspoon dried oregano
Ground black pepper

Place 1 cup of feta in the bowl of a food processor; process to a fine texture. Add cream cheese, oregano and pepper; process until smooth. Scrape into a bowl; stir in remaining feta. Transfer to a serving bowl or storage container.

Olive, Lemon and Thyme Spread

Makes about 1 cup

2 medium garlic cloves, peeled
1/4 cup fresh parsley
1/2 teaspoon dried thyme leaves
1/4 teaspoon finely grated lemon zest

2 tablespoons juice from a lemon
2 tablespoons extra virgin olive oil
1-1/4 cups pimento-stuffed olives from a 10-ounce jar, drained

Place garlic, parsley and thyme in the bowl of a food processor; process until finely minced. Add lemon zest and juice, olive oil and olives; pulse until olives are chopped to a fine gravel texture. Transfer to a serving bowl or storage container.

White Bean Dip with Roasted Garlic Gremolata

Makes 12 to 15 servings

12 garlic cloves, unpeeled

1 (16 ounce) can cannellini beans

1/3 cup packed Italian parsley, chopped, rinsed and drained

1 (2x1/4-inch) lemon peel strip, chopped

3 tablespoons lemon juice

1 tablespoon olive oil

1/4 teaspoon salt

Freshly ground pepper

Preheat oven to 400 degrees F. Place garlic in a pie plate. Drizzle with olive oil. Roast until soft, but not brown, about 15 minutes. Cool slightly, then trim ends and peel. Mince parsley and lemon peel in processor. Add roasted garlic, beans, lemon juice, oil, and salt. Season with pepper; process until smooth. Transfer to a serving bowl. Can be prepared a day ahead. Cover and refrigerate. Bring to room temperature before serving.

Caponata

Makes 3 cups

3 cups peeled, cubed eggplant

1/4 cup olive oil

1/2 cup chopped green pepper

1/2 cup chopped onion

1/2 cup chopped celery

1 cup canned tomatoes

1/4 cup sliced black olives

1/4 cup sliced green olives

1 tablespoon capers

1 tablespoon pine nuts

1/4 cup red wine vinegar

1 tablespoon or more to taste, sugar

1/2 teaspoon salt

1/2 teaspoon pepper

In a skillet, brown the eggplant in oil and stir in green pepper, onion and celery. Cook covered for 10 minutes. Do not let these ingredients brown. Add tomatoes, olives, capers, pine nuts, vinegar and sugar. Simmer, covered, for 30 minutes. Add salt and pepper. Chill. Caponata will keep for a few days in the refrigerator.

Sicilian Chickpeas with Cured Italian Meats

Makes 24 hors d'oeuvres

1 (15-ounce) can chickpeas, drained and rinsed

3/8 cup very thinly sliced heart of celery, including some chopped leaves

1/4 red onion, minced

2 tablespoons minced fresh Italian parsley

1/4 teaspoon dried hot pepper flakes

1 clove garlic, very finely minced

3 tablespoons extra virgin olive oil

1/2 tablespoon champagne vinegar

Sea salt to taste

Large platter of Italian cured meats, thinly sliced

24 water crackers or toasted sliced baguette

Combine chickpeas, celery, onion, parsley, hot pepper flakes, garlic, olive oil and vinegar; toss well. Season to taste with salt. Serve immediately alongside a large platter of thinly sliced Italian cured meats (such as salami and prosciutto) with a basket of crackers.

Baked Olive Antipasto

Makes 12 servings

8 ounces mixed Italian olives, drained

1 (14-ounce) jar/can artichoke hearts, rinsed and chopped coarsely

1 (10-ounce) jar roasted peppers, drained and cut into thin strips

2 tablespoons olive oil

6 cloves fresh garlic, sliced thinly

2 teaspoons grated orange zest

1 teaspoon fresh thyme

4 ounces smoked mozzarella cheese, cubed

Preheat oven to 425 degrees F. Combine everything except cheese into shallow baking dish. Bake for 15 to 20 minutes. Remove from oven and let rest for 5 minutes. Stir in mozzarella. Bake in oven for 5 minutes. Serve with toasted bread.

Gathering Peppers, 1935, by Geronima Cruz Montoya, San Juan Pueblo, #52752/13. Museum of Indian Arts and Culture/Laboratory of Anthropology, Department of Cultural Affairs, www.miaclab.org. Photo by Blair Clark.

Roasted Prosciutto-Wrapped Asparagus

Makes about 40 pieces

2 pounds asparagus, about 40 spears
1 pound thinly sliced prosciutto, sliced in half lengthwise

Olive oil
Salt and freshly ground black pepper to taste
Lemon wedges or zest for garnish

Preheat oven to 400 degrees F. Blanch asparagus by plunging into a large pot of boiling water for about 3 minutes; remove while still crisp. (If desired, add a pinch of salt and baking soda to the water to help the asparagus keep its bright green color.) Stop cooking by transferring the asparagus to a bowl of ice water. Drain and let dry. Wrap each asparagus spear diagonally with a strip of prosciutto. Drizzle with olive oil. Sprinkle with salt and pepper to taste.

Antipasto

Makes 8 servings

24 ounces thinly sliced prosciutto
2 cups toasted almonds
48 niçoise olives or other small brined black pitted olives
1/4 cup olive oil

48 picholine olives or other pitted green olives
Olive oil
Salt and pepper to taste

Arrange sliced prosciutto on large serving platter. Scatter almonds and olives over. Drizzle with olive oil; sprinkle with salt and pepper.

Hummus

Makes 2-1/2 cups

1 (10-ounce) can garbanzo beans
1/2 cup yogurt
2 to 3 tablespoons lemon juice
2 to 3 tablespoons tahini paste
3 cloves garlic, minced

1/4 to 1/2 teaspoon ground cumin
4 tablespoons finely chopped parsley
Pita chips or raw vegetables

Drain garbanzo beans, saving some of the juice. Place beans, yogurt and lemon juice in a blender; puree. Add remaining ingredients, taking care to blend in the tahini paste, which tends to stick together. If too dry, add bean juice and/or lemon juice to achieve desired consistency. When serving, drizzle a little virgin olive oil on top. Serve with pita chips and fresh vegetables for dipping.

Eggplant-Chèvre Mousse

Makes about 4 cups

1 large eggplant (1-1/2 to 2 pounds)
Olive oil for coating
1 head garlic, roasted, pulp squeezed
 from the cloves
1 red bell pepper, roasted, peeled,
 seeded and finely diced
4 ounces unaged chèvre cheese
1 scallion, thinly sliced
2 tablespoons chopped fresh basil
 leaves

2 tablespoons chopped fresh
 cilantro leaves and stems
Juice of 1/2 lemon
2 teaspoons red wine vinegar
1/2 teaspoon ground cumin
1/4 teaspoon salt
1/4 teaspoon freshly ground
 black pepper

Preheat oven to 450 degrees F. Halve the eggplant lengthwise and rub the flesh with a little of the olive oil. Place the halves, cut sides down, on a baking sheet. Roast until very soft, about 20 minutes. Remove and let cool to room temperature. Scrape the eggplant pulp out of the skin with a large spoon. Discard the skin; very finely chop the pulp. Combine remaining ingredients in a large mixing bowl. Mash together with a fork until well combined. Taste for seasoning; depending upon how tangy the chèvre is, you might desire more salt or vinegar. Serve at room temperature with pita chips or cover and refrigerate for up to 4 days. If refrigerated, bring to room temperature before serving.

Roasted Garlic, Brie and Grape Crostini

Makes 24 crostinis

30 cloves garlic, peeled
1/2 cup olive oil
3/4 teaspoon thyme
2 cups seedless grapes, halved
 (red and green)
1/3 cup Ruby Port
3/4 teaspoon chopped fresh
 rosemary

Pinch sugar
1 baguette, cut diagonally into 24
 slices and toasted
8 ounces Brie cheese, rind removed,
 room temperature

Preheat oven to 325 degrees F. Combine garlic and oil in a small baking dish. Bake until garlic is tender, about 35 minutes. Drain, reserving 3 tablespoons oil. Transfer garlic to food processor. Add thyme and reserved oil and puree. Mix grapes, port, rosemary and sugar in a bowl and let stand 30 minutes. Spread each baguette slice with 1 teaspoon garlic. Spread 2 teaspoons cheese over and top with grape mixture.

Tapenade

Makes 1-1/2 cups

1 (6-ounce) can albacore tuna, drained
1/3 cup fresh lemon juice
1 (2-ounce) can flat anchovies, drained
1/4 cup capers, drained

1 (8-ounce) can pitted black olives
1 generous tablespoon cognac or brandy
1/4 cup olive oil
Freshly ground pepper to taste

Combine tuna, lemon juice, anchovies, capers, olives and brandy in a blender or food processor and whirl until smooth. With machine running, add olive oil in a slow, steady stream until mixture is thick and creamy. Season to taste with pepper. Transfer to serving bowl and surround with crudités. This will keep for a week in the refrigerator.

Olive Puffs

Makes 24 servings

1/2 cup butter (pack tightly to measure)
1 cup flour
2 cups grated sharp Cheddar cheese

1/8 to 1/4 teaspoon cayenne pepper, to taste
1 (7-ounce) jar stuffed green olives

Preheat oven to 400 degrees F. Allow both cheese and butter to soften. Mix butter, flour, cheese and cayenne pepper. Drain and dry olives. Wrap each olive with cheese mixture. Freeze individually on a cookie sheet. Transfer to a freezer bag. Keep frozen until ready to bake. Bake for 20 minutes.

Hot Olive Spread

Makes 20 servings

1 cup chopped black olives
3/4 cup mayonnaise
1/2 cup chopped green onions
1/2 teaspoon salt

1-1/2 cups shredded sharp Cheddar cheese
1/2 teaspoon curry powder
Toasted bread rounds

Preheat oven to 350 degrees F. Mix all ingredients well. Spread mixture on bread rounds. Bake 10 minutes or until brown and bubbly. Serve hot. This spread may be stored for 2 to 3 weeks in the refrigerator.

Spiced Olives

Makes 20 servings

1 cup olive oil
1/4 cup water
1/2 cup white wine
3 cloves garlic
2 bay leaves
3 dried whole chiles
1/2 teaspoon dried oregano

Coarsely ground black pepper
  to taste
3 thick lemon slices
1 cup each of Greek, Spanish and
  Italian olives (drained and seeded)
1 full branch thyme
Fresh thyme for garnish

In a saucepan, combine the oil, water and wine. Heat to just boiling and remove from stove. Add the seasonings and let stand for 30 minutes. In a glass container, put the lemons in the bottom and cover with the olives. Pour the liquid mixture over the olives and seal with a lid. Marinate at least a day ahead. Serve in a flat bowl garnished with the fresh thyme.

Green Olive Spread

Makes 8 servings

1 cup chopped green olives
  (Sicilian, pitted)
1/2 cup chopped parsley
1/2 cup chopped onion
3 tablespoons lemon juice

1/2 cup chopped pine nuts or
  walnuts
1/2 cup chopped green onions
1/3 cup olive oil
1/4 teaspoon red pepper

Combine all ingredients in a food processor. Using about 5 on/off turns, process just until mixture holds together (do not puree). Transfer to a small bowl. Season with salt and pepper. Can be prepared 1 day ahead. Cover and refrigerate.

Olive-Caper Spread

Makes 8 servings

1 cup Greek olives, pitted
5 tablespoons olive oil
2 tablespoons fresh basil, chopped

3 tablespoons capers, drained
5 cloves garlic, minced

In a food processor, puree all ingredients. Set aside until ready to serve. Mixture may be refrigerated for up to 3 days. Bring it back to room temperature before serving with crackers or toast.

Marinated Mushrooms

Makes 20 to 24 servings

1 pound fresh button mushrooms,
   stems removed
3/4 cup wine vinegar
1/4 cup water
1/2 cup oil
1 bay leaf, broken

1 teaspoon crushed fennel seeds
1/4 teaspoon salt
1/8 teaspoon pepper
1 clove garlic, minced
1 to 2 teaspoons finely
   chopped parsley

Combine all ingredients except mushrooms, garlic and parsley and boil 5 minutes. Put mushrooms into a large jar or bowl and pour boiled mixture over. Stir well. Add garlic. Stir to blend. Cover and refrigerate at least 12 hours. Drain and sprinkle with parsley. Serve with toothpicks.

Smoked Cheese Squares

Makes 25 to 30 squares

2 medium onions, sliced
2 tablespoons butter
1 tablespoon olive oil
1-1/2 tablespoons brown sugar
1 tablespoon balsamic vinegar
1/2 cup pitted whole dates, chopped
1/3 cup pine nuts

3/4 cup shredded mozzarella cheese
3/4 cup shredded smoked Gouda
   cheese
1/2 cup shredded Cheddar cheese
1 (16-ounce) Italian bread shell
   (Boboli)

Preheat oven to 450 degrees F. In a large skillet, cook the onions in butter and oil over medium heat for 10 to 12 minutes, stirring occasionally. Stir in sugar, vinegar and dates. Cook and stir 5 minutes more, or until onions are golden brown. Remove from heat and stir in pine nuts. In a bowl, combine all cheeses, and sprinkle evenly over the bread shell. Top with onion mixture. Place bread shell on an ungreased baking sheet. Bake for 8 to 10 minutes, until cheese is melted. Let stand 5 minutes, and then cut into 2-inch squares.

Roquefort and Bacon Pinwheels

Makes 10 to 12 pinwheels

1 sheet frozen puff pastry, thawed
4 to 5 ounces Roquefort bleu
   cheese

5 slices bacon, cooked crisp and
   crumbled
1 large egg, slightly beaten with
   1 teaspoon of water

Preheat oven to 400 degrees F. Butter a 9-inch baking dish. Open the sheet of puff pastry and flatten with a rolling pin. Crumble the bleu cheese on the sheet, leaving a 1-inch border all around. Sprinkle with bacon crumbs. Roll up the pastry the long way and cut into 10 to 12 slices, 1/2 inch thick. Place the rounds on a prepared dish. Brush with egg wash. Bake 10 to 14 minutes, until puffed and golden brown. Serve.

Marinated Cheese

Makes 4 to 6 servings

5 to 7 ounces manchego cheese
   wedge
6 tablespoons olive oil
1 tablespoon white wine vinegar
1 teaspoon black or green
   peppercorns

1 large clove garlic, sliced thinly
Fresh tarragon and fresh thyme
   sprigs, broken into small pieces

Cut cheese into 1/2- to 3/4-inch cubes. Mix together remaining ingredients. Put all together in a small bowl and mix well. Cover and chill at least 2 to 3 days, inverting and remixing the cheese periodically to blend. When ready to eat, drain oil and serve with toothpicks, saving oil for restorage (if any cheese remains). Will keep at least 2 weeks in the refrigerator.

Pueblo Crafts, 1938, by Geronima Cruz Montoya, San Juan Pueblo, #54002/13. Museum of Indian Arts and Culture/Laboratory of Anthropology, Department of Cultural Affairs, www.miaclab.org. Photo by Blair Clark.

Dips and Spreads

Goat Cheese Gratin

Makes 6 servings

10 ounces soft goat cheese, crumbled

2 teaspoons minced fresh rosemary leaves

2 teaspoons minced fresh oregano leaves or a pinch of dried-leaf oregano, crushed

1-1/2 to 2 cups homemade tomato sauce, room temperature

24 best-quality black olives, pitted

Preheat broiler. Scatter the cheese on the bottom of a 10-1/2-inch round baking dish. Sprinkle with half of the herbs. Spoon on just enough tomato sauce to evenly coat the cheese. Sprinkle with olives and the remaining herbs. Place baking dish under the broiler about 3 inches from the heat. Broil about 2 to 3 minutes, until the cheese is melted and fragrant, and the tomato sauce is sizzling. Serve with Melba rounds or bagel chips.

This is a simple dish with a big taste. This dish lends itself to endless variations. Think of it simply as a pizza without the crust. Add julienned bits of prosciutto, a bit of cooked sausage, sautéed mushrooms or marinated artichokes.

Perfectly Pesto Cheesecake

Makes 18 servings

CRUST

1 tablespoon softened butter

1/4 cup fine, dry breadcrumbs

2 tablespoons grated Parmesan cheese

FILLING

2 (8-ounce) packages cream cheese, room temperature

1 cup ricotta cheese

1/2 cup grated Parmesan cheese

1/2 teaspoon salt

1/8 teaspoon cayenne pepper

3 large eggs

1/2 cup pesto sauce

1/2 cup pine nuts

Preheat oven to 325 degrees F. Rub butter over bottom and sides of a 9-inch-diameter springform pan. Mix breadcrumbs with 2 tablespoons grated Parmesan. Coat pan with crumb mixture. Using an electric mixer, beat cream cheese, ricotta, 1/2 cup Parmesan cheese, salt and cayenne until light and well blended. Add eggs, one at a time, beating well after each addition. Transfer half the mixture to a medium bowl. Mix pesto into remaining half. Pour pesto mixture into a prepared pan; smooth top. Carefully smooth plain cheese mixture over pesto mixture. Gently smooth top. Sprinkle with pine nuts and bake cheesecake until center no longer moves when pan is shaken, about 45 minutes. Transfer to a rack and cool completely. Run a small, sharp knife around sides of pan to loosen cheesecake. Release pan sides from cheesecake. Transfer to a platter and garnish with fresh basil sprigs. Surround with crackers and serve.

Note: To keep pesto from turning black on top when stored, pour a thin film of olive oil over the surface, cover and refrigerate.

Baked Brie with Blueberry Ginger Topping

Makes 10 to 12 servings

1-1/2 cups fresh blueberries

1/3 cup firmly packed light brown sugar

1-1/2 tablespoons cornstarch

2 tablespoons cider vinegar

1-1/2 tablespoons grated fresh ginger

1 (3-inch) stick cinnamon

1/8 teaspoon salt

1 (8-ounce) Brie cheese round

Preheat oven to 350 degrees F. Combine first 7 ingredients in a large saucepan. Bring to a boil over medium heat and cook for 3 to 5 minutes. Remove cinnamon stick. Cover and chill blueberry mixture for 2 hours. Place Brie on an ungreased baking sheet. Bake at 350 degrees F for 8 to 10 minutes or until soft. Transfer cheese to a serving plate and top evenly with blueberry mixture. Serve with crackers.

Brie Strata with Apricot-Papaya Salsa

Makes 10 to 12 servings

1 cup apricot nectar

3/4 cup quartered dried apricots

2 cups diced peeled papaya

1 tablespoon honey

1 tablespoon fresh lime juice

1 (15-ounce) Brie cheese round

8 cups (1-inch) cubes French bread

Vegetable cooking spray

2 tablespoons brown sugar

1 (12-ounce) can evaporated skim milk

1/4 teaspoon salt

3 egg whites, lightly beaten

2 eggs, lightly beaten

Preheat oven to 350 degrees F. Combine the nectar and apricots in a microwave-safe bowl. Microwave on high for 2 minutes, or until mixture boils. Cover and let stand for 30 minutes, or until apricots soften. Drain apricots, reserving 2 tablespoons of nectar; discard remaining nectar. Combine apricots, reserved nectar, papaya, honey and lime juice. Stir gently and set salsa aside. Remove rind from Brie and discard. Cut Brie into small pieces. Arrange bread cubes in the bottom of a 9-inch-square baking dish coated with cooking spray. Top with half of Brie, and sprinkle with half of brown sugar. Repeat procedure with remaining bread, Brie and brown sugar. Combine milk, salt, egg whites and eggs. Stir well. Pour over bread and press firmly with back of spoon to moisten all bread cubes. Cover and chill 30 minutes. Bake in oven for 20 to 30 minutes, or until eggs have set and Brie is melting.

Camembert Sauté

Makes 4 servings

1 Camembert cheese round

2 eggs, beaten

1 cup cracker crumbs

4 tablespoons butter

2 chopped green onions

Dip cheese in eggs, then cracker crumbs, and sauté in butter. Turn; sauté until cheese starts to run. Remove to plate. Add more butter to skillet and rest of crumbs and green onions; sauté. Place on top of cheese and serve with rice crackers.

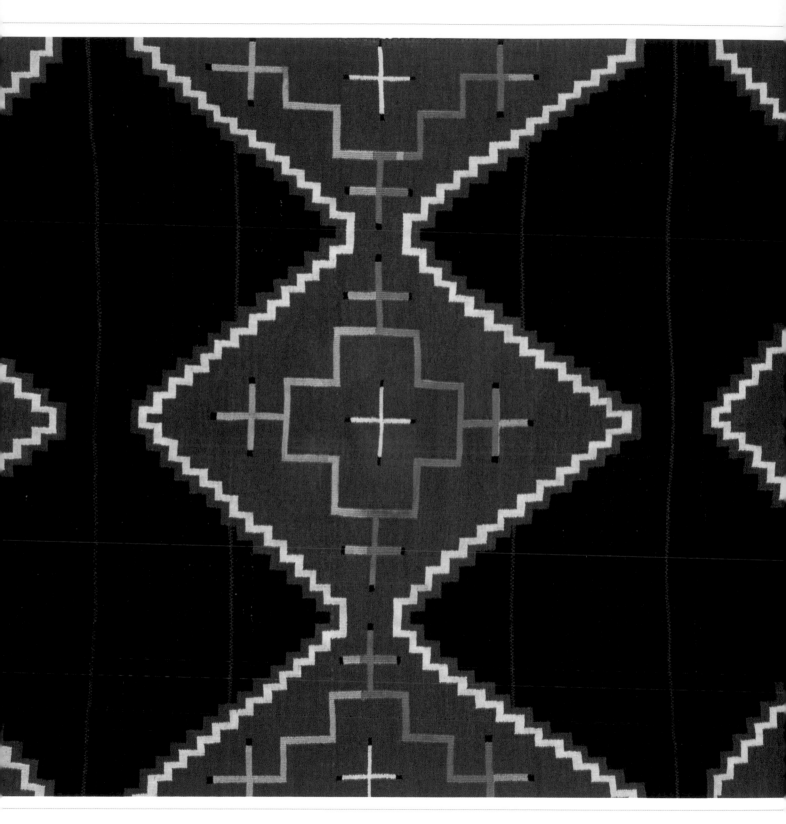

Navajo Chief's Blanket 3rd Phase Variant, 1880–1890, 09114/12. *Museum of Indian Arts and Culture/Laboratory of Anthropology, Department of Cultural Affairs, www.miaclab.org. Photo by Blair Clark.*

Cranberry-Glazed Brie

CRANBERRY MARMALADE

3 cups cranberries
3/4 cup firmly packed golden brown
 sugar
1/3 cup dried currants
1/3 cup water
1/8 teaspoon dry mustard
1/8 teaspoon ground allspice
1/8 teaspoon ground cardamom
1/8 teaspoon ground cloves
1/8 teaspoon ground ginger

1 (8-inch) Brie round

Preheat oven to 350 degrees F. For marmalade, combine all ingredients in a heavy nonaluminum saucepan. Cook over medium-high heat about 5 minutes, stirring frequently until most of the berries pop. Cool mixture to room temperature. (Can be prepared 3 days ahead. Cover tightly and refrigerate.)

For cheese, using a sharp knife, cut a circle in top rind, leaving 1/2-inch border of rind. Carefully remove center circle of rind from cheese. Do not cut through side rind. Place cheese in an 8-inch-diameter ceramic baking dish or on a baking sheet lined with foil. Spread cranberry marmalade over cheese. Bake cheese until soft, about 12 minutes. Let cool slightly. Set cheese on a large platter. Surround with crackers and apple and pear slices. Serve warm or at room temperature.

Chutney Cheese Ball

Makes 10 servings

11 ounces softened cream cheese
3 tablespoons golden raisins
3 tablespoons sour cream
3 teaspoons curry powder
3/4 cup chopped roasted peanuts
 or cashews

1/2 cup chutney
4 tablespoons crisp, cooked,
 crumbled bacon
1 tablespoon minced onion
1/4 cup toasted coconut
Green onion brushes

Mix all ingredients except coconut. Chill for 1 hour or until firm enough to shape into a ball. When ready to serve, roll in toasted coconut and garnish with green onion brushes. Can be prepared one day ahead.

Dill, Feta and Garlic Cream Cheese Spread

Makes 24 servings

2 (8-ounce) packages softened or
 room-temperature cream cheese
1 (8-ounce) package crumbled feta
 cheese

3 cloves garlic, peeled and minced
2 tablespoons chopped fresh dill

In a medium bowl, thoroughly blend all ingredients with an electric mixer. Cover and refrigerate for at least 4 hours. Serve with firm, raw veggies or with crackers.

Curried Cheese Spread

6 ounces cream cheese
8 ounces sharp Cheddar cheese
3 tablespoons sherry
1/2 teaspoon curry

1/4 teaspoon salt
10 ounces chutney
1/4 cup minced green onions

Mix all ingredients except chutney and onions with an electric mixer. Spread in a shallow dish and chill until firm. Before serving, spread chopped chutney over cheese mixture and cover with green onions. Serve with wheat crackers.

Hot Onion Soufflé

1 cup mayonnaise
1 cup grated fresh Parmesan cheese
1 cup minced Vidalia onions

Preheat oven to 350 degrees F. Mix all ingredients and bake until slightly bubbly. Serve with crackers, toast rounds or chips.

Pecan Cheese Spread

3/4 cup mayonnaise
1/2 cup finely chopped, lightly toasted pecans
2 tablespoons finely chopped green onions

1/4 pound bacon, crumbled
2 cups of coarsely grated Cheddar cheese

In a bowl, stir together mayonnaise, pecans, onions and bacon until combined well. Stir in cheese until combined well. Pack mixture into a small serving bowl or crock. Cover and chill at least 2 hours. Serve spread at room temperature with crackers or bread.

Pimiento Cheese

3 to 4 cups grated Cheddar cheese
1 (2-ounce) jar of whole drained pimientos
1 cup mayonnaise, divided
1/8 teaspoon onion powder

1/8 teaspoon ground red pepper
1 to 2 dashes Worcestershire sauce
1/2 cup chopped green chiles
2 to 3 tablespoons sugar

In a food processor fitted with a metal blade, add the cheese and pimientos. Pulse several times to combine. Add 3/4 cup of the mayonnaise and pulse again. Add onion powder, red pepper, Worcestershire sauce, green chiles and sugar and pulse several times until well blended. Add remaining mayonnaise and pulse until mixture reaches desired consistency. Keep in the refrigerator until ready to serve.

Chunky Cheese Spread

Makes 15 servings

3 cups grated, sharp Cheddar cheese

1 cup chopped pecans

4 chopped green onions

1 cup mayonnaise

1 (8-ounce) jar jalapeño jelly

Mix cheese, pecans, onions and mayonnaise. Spread in dish or platter so it is 1/2 inch thick. Use a dish that you will serve it in. Let stand in refrigerator overnight. When ready to serve, top with jelly and serve with whole grain crackers.

Hungarian Cheese Spread

Makes 6 servings

1 (8-ounce) package cream cheese

1/4 cup sour cream

1/4 cup softened butter

2 teaspoons anchovy paste

2 teaspoons drained capers

2 chopped shallots

1/8 teaspoon salt

1 tablespoon paprika

1/8 teaspoon dry mustard

1 ounce ale or beer

1/4 teaspoon caraway seeds

Mix all ingredients well in a blender. Pour in a bowl and refrigerate several hours. Serve with crackers.

Curry Almond Cheese Spread

Makes 3 cups

2 (8-ounce) packages softened cream cheese

1 (9-ounce) jar mango chutney

1 cup toasted slivered almonds

1 tablespoon curry powder

1/2 teaspoon dry mustard

Toasted almonds for garnish

Fresh cranberries for garnish

Parsley for garnish

Process all ingredients, except garnishes, in a food processor until smooth, stopping to scrape down sides. Cover and chill 1 hour. Shape mixture into a round. Chill until ready to serve. Sprinkle with more toasted almonds, fresh cranberries, and parsley sprigs for garnish. Serve with Granny Smith apples.

Peanut Butter Canapés

3 ounces cream cheese

1/2 cup peanut butter

4 ounces Major Grey's Chutney, cut
  into small pieces

1/2 teaspoon Lawry's Seasoned Salt

1/4 teaspoon Lea & Perrins
  Worcestershire sauce

Dry red wine

Mix and blend the ingredients, then add dry red wine until mixture is a good spreading consistency. Best served on Triscuits. Keeps for weeks in a covered jar in the refrigerator.

Blue Cheese Spread

Makes 6 (2-tablespoon) servings

1/4 cup mayonnaise

3 tablespoons fat-free sour cream

1 tablespoon buttermilk

1 teaspoon Dijon mustard

1/4 teaspoon Worcestershire sauce

3/4 cup crumbled blue cheese

Salt and pepper to taste

In a small bowl, stir together mayonnaise, sour cream, buttermilk, mustard and Worcestershire sauce. Stir in blue cheese until mixture is almost smooth. Season to taste with salt and pepper. If desired, cover and refrigerate for up to 3 days. Serve with celery sticks and apple and/or pear slices.

Bacon and Blue Cheese Dip

Makes 2 to 3 cups

8 slices chopped bacon

3 cloves garlic minced

8 ounces softened cream cheese

1/3 cup heavy cream

1 cup crumbled blue cheese

3 tablespoons fresh chopped chives

3 tablespoons chopped smoked
  almonds

Preheat oven to 350 degrees F. Cook bacon in a large skillet over medium heat until almost crisp. Drain off excess fat. Add garlic and cook about 4 minutes longer. Beat cream cheese and heavy cream until blended and smooth. Add bacon mixture, blue cheese and chives. Blend, then pour mixture into a small baking dish and bake about 30 minutes. Remove from oven, sprinkle with almonds and serve with favorite crackers, toasted bread or vegetables.

Photo by Peter Vitale

Royal Blue Dip

Makes 6 servings

1/2 pound crumbled good quality
    blue cheese

1/3 cup chopped onion

1/3 cup extra virgin olive oil

1 tablespoon fresh lemon juice

1 tablespoon red wine vinegar

1/2 teaspoon crushed fresh garlic

1 teaspoon Dijon mustard

1/4 teaspoon coarse ground black
    pepper

1/4 cup chopped fresh parsley

Spread crumbled cheese in 9-inch pie plate. Combine rest of ingredients, except for parsley, in a food processor. Pulse 3 or 4 times. Pour over cheese and sprinkle with parsley. Let stand for 2 hours. Serve with crudités, small toasts or party crackers.

Hot Asiago Dip

Makes 4 cups

1 cup mayonnaise

1 cup sour cream

1/3 to 1/2 cup sliced mushrooms

1/3 cup chopped green onions

1/3 cup chopped black or pimento-
    stuffed olives

1/2 cup chopped sun-dried tomatoes

1-1/2 cups shredded Asiago cheese

Preheat oven to 350 degrees F. Combine all ingredients in a bowl (can be done 24 hours ahead). To serve, transfer mixture to ovenproof dish and bake for 15 to 20 minutes, or until warmed through. Top with additional green onion and serve with baguette slices or crackers.

Reuben Dip

Makes 10 servings

1 (14-ounce) can drained, slightly
    chopped sauerkraut

1 (6-ounce) package chopped corned
    beef

8 ounces shredded Swiss cheese

1/2 cup shredded Cheddar cheese

3/4 to 1 cup mayonnaise to desired
    consistency

Preheat oven to 350 degrees F. Combine all ingredients and spread evenly in an 8 x 8-inch baking dish. Bake uncovered 25 to 30 minutes. Serve warm with bread pieces or rye Melba toast. Can also be served in hollowed-out rye or pumpernickel bread.

Chef's Choice Vegetable Dip

Makes about 2 cups

1 cup Hellmann's mayonnaise
(no substitute)

1/2 cup sour cream

1/2 teaspoon crushed oregano

1/2 teaspoon crushed dried basil

1/4 teaspoon crushed dried thyme

1/4 teaspoon salt

1/8 teaspoon curry powder

2 teaspoons chopped and drained
capers

1-1/2 teaspoons fresh lemon juice

1-1/2 teaspoons Worcestershire sauce

1 tablespoon grated onion

1 tablespoon fresh, chopped parsley

Blend all ingredients in a small bowl. Cover and refrigerate until serving time. Serve with fresh celery, grape tomatoes, strips of red pepper, green onions, cucumbers, zucchini slices, blanched cauliflower, broccoli and carrot pieces. To blanch: bring water to a boil in a saucepan. Have a deep bowl ready with ice cubes and ice water. Drop prepared vegetables into boiling water for only 2 to 3 minutes. Time carefully. Dip out vegetables with a slotted spoon and plunge them into ice water. Remove with slotted spoon to drain on paper towels. Repeat with remaining vegetables (they will be easier to eat and retain their bright colors).

Crudités with Creamy Pistachio Dip

Makes 40 servings

2 cups unsalted, raw, shelled
pistachio nuts

1 very large shallot, minced

1/4 cup plus 1 tablespoon champagne
vinegar

1 generous cup mayonnaise

2 tablespoons fresh lemon juice

1 large clove garlic, minced

1/2 cup plus 1 tablespoon extra virgin
olive oil

2 cups crème fraîche

1/3 cup minced Italian parsley

2 tablespoons minced fresh
tarragon

Salt and pepper to taste

Assorted vegetables for dipping:
cucumbers, radishes, endive,
carrots

Preheat oven to 375 degrees F. Spread pistachios on a baking sheet and bake until toasted (8 to 10 minutes), or toast in a skillet over medium heat in 2 batches. Let nuts cool, and then transfer to a food processor and pulse until coarsely ground. In a small bowl, soak the shallots in the vinegar for 15 minutes. In a large bowl, whisk the mayonnaise with the lemon juice and garlic. Gradually whisk in the olive oil until thickened. Drain the shallots and stir into mayonnaise along with the crème fraîche, parsley and tarragon. Stir in pistachios and season with salt and pepper. Pour into serving bowls and serve with crudités or crackers.

Pepperoni Pizza Dip

Makes 16 servings

8 ounces ricotta cheese

3/4 cup mayonnaise

1-1/2 cups shredded mozzarella cheese, separated

1/4 cup grated Parmesan cheese

1/2 cup finely chopped pepperoni

1 teaspoon garlic powder

1 teaspoon Italian seasoning

1/8 teaspoon crushed red pepper

Preheat oven to 350 degrees F. Combine ricotta, mayonnaise and 1/2 cup mozzarella in a medium-size bowl. Stir in Parmesan, pepperoni, garlic powder, Italian seasoning and red pepper. Mix well and spoon into an ungreased ovenproof 1 1/2-quart casserole dish. Sprinkle remaining cup of mozzarella on top. Bake for 25 to 30 minutes or until cheese is bubbly and golden. Serve hot with wedges of Italian bread. Garnish with chopped black olives and cherry tomato halves.

Polynesian Ginger Dip

Makes 12 servings

1 cup mayonnaise

1 cup sour cream

1/4 cup finely chopped onion

1/4 cup minced parsley

1/4 cup finely chopped water chestnuts

2 tablespoons chopped candied ginger

2 cloves minced garlic

1 tablespoon soy sauce

Combine all ingredients and let set several hours to allow flavors to develop. Serve with sesame seed crackers, sesame bread wafers or potato chips. Substitute cream cheese for half of the sour cream and mayonnaise so it will "set up" more than a dip. Serve on a toast square topped by a shrimp split lengthwise that has been cooked with a dash of soy sauce and sesame oil.

Layered Chicken Curry Dip

Makes 10 servings

1 (8-ounce) package cream cheese

1 cup cottage cheese

1/4 cup sour cream

2 teaspoons curry powder

1/2 cup chutney

1/3 cup chopped green onions

1/3 cup chopped raisins

1/3 cup shredded coconut

1 cup chopped cooked chicken

1/2 cup chopped salted peanuts

In a food processor, combine cream cheese, cottage cheese, sour cream and curry powder. Process until smooth. Spread mixture on the bottom of a platter or quiche dish. Top with chutney, green onions, raisins, coconut, chicken and peanuts, in that order. Cover and refrigerate 3 to 4 hours or overnight. Serve with assorted crackers.

Taos Pueblo–Moonlight, *1914, by E. Irving Couse, oil on canvas, 60 x 60 inches. Collections of the New Mexico Museum of Art, gift of Kibbey W. Couse, 1930. Photo by Blair Clark.*

Sun-Dried Tomato Torte

Makes 12 servings

1 (8-ounce) package softened cream cheese

1/2 cup crumbled feta cheese

1 tablespoon milk

3 cloves garlic, minced

1 cup firmly packed basil leaves

1 cup firmly packed parsley leaves

3/4 cup Parmesan cheese

2 cloves garlic, minced

1/4 cup pine nuts

3 tablespoons olive oil

4 tablespoons toasted pine nuts

1/2 cup drained and diced oil-packed sun-dried tomatoes

Filling: combine cream cheese, feta, milk and 3 cloves garlic in a blender until smooth.

Pesto: combine basil, parsley, Parmesan cheese, 2 cloves garlic, 1/4 cup pine nuts and olive oil in a blender. Pulse until almost smooth, stopping machine several times and scraping sides.

To Assemble: Line a 4-cup mold with plastic wrap. Sprinkle toasted pine nuts over bottom of mold. Spread a fourth of the filling evenly over the nuts. Carefully spread half of the pesto on top. Add another fourth of filling. Sprinkle with tomatoes. Add remaining layer of filling, followed by a layer of remaining pesto. Cover and chill overnight. To serve, unmold onto a serving platter. Serve with crackers.

Petite Tomato Canapés

Makes 10 to 12 servings

40 rinsed and dried large ripe cherry tomatoes

4 ounces room-temperature cream cheese

1/2 pound smoked salmon

2 tablespoons fresh lemon juice

1 tablespoon minced onion

Whipping cream

Salt and pepper to taste

Fresh dill for garnish

Capers for garnish

Watercress or parsley for garnish

Using a knife with serrated edge, cut across tomatoes at stem end. Using small end of a melon scoop, carefully hollow out seeds and pulp, leaving 1/4-inch shells. Turn tomatoes upside down on paper towels to drain. Place cream cheese in a medium bowl and add salmon, lemon juice and onion. Mix lightly. Add enough cream to give a smooth consistency and blend well. Add salt and pepper, if needed. Using a small spoon or pastry bag with large star tip, fill tomatoes with salmon pâté, mounding mixture slightly. Put sprig of dill and a caper on top of each. Arrange canapés on a platter and garnish with watercress or parsley. Can be made a day ahead covered in plastic wrap in the refrigerator.

White Bean with Garlic and Rosemary Spread

Makes about 1 cup

2 tablespoons olive oil, plus extra for drizzling

2 medium garlic cloves, peeled

2 tablespoons minced fresh rosemary

1 (16-ounce) can undrained white beans

Place olive oil, garlic and rosemary in a 10-inch skillet. Heat pan until ingredients start to sizzle. Add beans and their liquid to the pan. As beans cook, mash them with a wooden spoon or potato masher. Cook until mixture is a loose spread consistency (it will thicken as it cools). Transfer to a serving bowl or storage container.

Onion Olé

Makes 8 servings

1 package Pillsbury hot roll mix

3 teaspoons frozen or dried chopped chives

1 egg

1 cup mayonnaise or salad dressing

1 pound grated Cheddar cheese

1 cup chopped green onions

2 teaspoons capers, if desired

1/2 cup grated Parmesan cheese

Preheat oven to 375 degrees F. Prepare hot roll mix as directed on package, adding chives along with egg. Cover and let rise in a warm place until doubled in size, 30 to 45 minutes. Roll out or pat dough to fit a greased 15 x 10-inch jelly roll pan. Combine mayonnaise, cheese, onions and capers. Spread mayonnaise mixture over dough in pan to within 1 inch of edges. Sprinkle top with Parmesan cheese. Bake for 30 to 45 minutes, until bubbling and golden brown. Cut in squares and serve at once.

Hot Artichoke Spread

Makes 4 cups

1 (14-ounce) can drained, chopped artichoke hearts

4 ounces chopped green chiles

1 cup mayonnaise

1 cup grated fresh Parmesan cheese

Dash of salt and garlic powder

Preheat oven to 350 degrees F. Mix all ingredients and pour into a small baking dish. Heat for 20 minutes or until bubbly. Serve with bread sticks, crackers or French bread.

Photo by Peter Vitale

Spinach Puffs

Makes 6 to 8 servings

3/4 cup all-purpose flour

1 teaspoon baking powder

1/2 teaspoon salt

1/2 teaspoon onion powder

1 (12-ounce) package defrosted, frozen spinach soufflé

1 egg, lightly beaten

3/4 cup shredded Swiss cheese

1/4 cup fine dry breadcrumbs

Vegetable oil

Grated Parmesan cheese

Sift flour with baking powder, salt and onion powder. Combine spinach soufflé and egg in medium bowl; add flour mixture, stirring well to combine. Add Swiss cheese and breadcrumbs; stir well to combine. Chill mixture for 30 minutes. Heat 3 inches of vegetable oil in a large skillet to 350 degrees F. Drop spinach mixture by rounded tablespoons into hot oil and fry for 2 minutes, or until golden brown. Drain on paper towels. Dust lightly with Parmesan cheese. Serve hot.

Seafood Appetizers

In the Mountains, 1935, by Ben Quintana, Cochiti Pueblo, #51418/13. Museum of Indian Arts and Culture/Laboratory of Anthropology, Department of Cultural Affairs, www.miaclab.org. Photo by Blair Clark.

Lemon-Fennel Shrimp with Tarragon

Makes 8 servings

1-1/2 pounds medium raw shrimp

2 tablespoons fresh lemon juice

3 tablespoons crushed fennel seeds

1/8 teaspoon dried red pepper flakes

Salt and pepper to taste

9 tablespoons olive oil

4 to 5 large cloves garlic, crushed

1 lemon, sliced thinly

3 tablespoons finely chopped tarragon leaves

Tarragon sprigs for garnish

In a large saucepan of salted water, bring to boil and cook shrimp 2 to 3 minutes, until opaque. Drain in colander and rinse under cold water until cool. Shell and devein shrimp. In another bowl whisk together lemon juice, fennel seeds, red pepper flakes and salt and pepper to taste. Add the oil in a thin stream, whisking. Stir in shrimp, garlic and sliced lemon and marinate overnight. Stir in chopped tarragon before serving and garnish with tarragon sprigs.

Sesame Shrimp Toasts with Chile Dipping Sauce

Makes 4 to 6 servings

CHILE DIPPING SAUCE

1/2 cup Thai sweet chile sauce

1 tablespoon soy sauce

1/2 teaspoon diced ginger

1 clove garlic, minced

2 tablespoons minced scallions

SHRIMP TOASTS

1/3 pound peeled, deveined, dry, chilled fresh shrimp

1/4 teaspoon minced fresh ginger

1/2 egg yolk

1 teaspoon soy sauce

4 tablespoons very cold heavy cream

1 teaspoon chopped cilantro (stems and all)

1/4 teaspoon kosher salt

1/4 teaspoon freshly ground black pepper

Firm, day-old white bread sliced 1/8 inch thick (crusts removed)

2 tablespoons white sesame seeds mixed with 2 tablespoons black sesame seeds

2 cups canola oil

Whisk all Chile Dipping Sauce ingredients thoroughly and refrigerate until needed.

Place shrimp, ginger, egg yolk and soy sauce in a food processor. Pulse until a rough paste is formed. At full speed, drizzle in cream until mixed. Add cilantro, salt and pepper and pulse a couple times. Spread mixture 1/4 inch thick evenly onto one side of bread slices (all the way to edges). Spread sesame seeds onto paste. Refrigerate at least 20 minutes. Heat canola oil to 350 degrees F in a deep skillet. Fry shrimp toasts for about 3 minutes or until white sesame seeds are lightly browned. Remove and drain on paper towels. Serve immediately with Chile Dipping Sauce.

Shrimp Dip

Makes 10 servings

2 cups grated Cheddar cheese

1 (12-ounce) can small cooked shrimp
  or fresh bay shrimp

1 can chopped water chestnuts

1 cup mayonnaise

1/4 cup sour cream

1/4 cup chopped onion

Dash hot pepper sauce

Mix all ingredients together and chill for flavors to meld. Serve with crackers.

Dill Shrimp

Makes 15 servings

1/2 cup sour cream

1/3 cup fresh lemon juice

1/4 cup sugar

1 large red onion, sliced thin

2 tablespoons dill weed

3 pounds cooked shrimp

Mix together first 5 ingredients. Add shrimp and refrigerate overnight. Serve cold with toothpicks or forks.

Grilled Cumin Shrimp

Makes 10 servings

8 tablespoons sweet butter

2 teaspoons ground turmeric

1-1/2 teaspoons ground cumin

1 teaspoon ground coriander

1-1/2 teaspoons salt

Juice of 2 lemons

2 pounds shelled and deveined
  large shrimp

Preheat broiler. Melt butter in a saucepan. Stir in turmeric, cumin coriander, salt and lemon juice. Arrange shrimp in a single layer in a shallow baking dish. Spread butter mixture over them. Broil under a very hot broiler until the shrimp are glazed and golden brown, about 8 minutes. Skewer with toothpicks and serve at once. May also be prepared on an outside grill. Do not overcook.

Shrimp Remoulade

Makes 10 servings

3/4 cup olive oil

1/4 cup prepared mustard

1/4 cup wine vinegar

1 teaspoon salt

1/2 teaspoon paprika

1 hard-boiled egg, chopped

1/2 cup minced celery

1 tablespoon grated onion

2 tablespoons minced parsley

2 tablespoons capers

1-1/2 to 2 pounds cooked and
  deveined shrimp

Whip the oil, mustard, vinegar, salt and paprika thoroughly. Fold in egg, celery, onion, parsley and capers. Add shrimp and chill for several hours. Serve with toothpicks.

The War Bonnet, *n.d., by E. Irving Couse, oil on canvas, 24-1/8 x 29 inches. Collections of the New Mexico Museum of Art, gift of Kibbey W. Couse, 1930. Photo by Blair Clark.*

Shrimp Curry Spread with Chutney

Makes 8 servings

1/2 pound peeled and cooked
   medium shrimp
8 ounces cream cheese
1 cup grated Cheddar cheese
2 tablespoons mayonnaise

1 clove garlic, minced
1 to 2 teaspoons curry powder
3/4 cup chopped chutney
4 to 5 green onions, chopped

Chop cooked shrimp. Mix cheeses and mayonnaise together. Add chopped shrimp, garlic and curry powder. Line bowl with plastic wrap and press cheese mixture into bowl to form a disc. Refrigerate overnight. To serve, remove plastic wrap and place formed cheese on a plate. Cover with chutney and sprinkle with chopped onions. Serve with crackers.

Crab and Avocado Fritters

Makes about 4 dozen fritters

1 pound crabmeat
1 cup diced green onions
1 medium avocado, peeled and cut
   into 1/4-inch pieces
2 eggs
1/2 cup hot chile salsa

1 teaspoon salt
1/4 cup dry breadcrumbs
Corn oil for deep frying
All-purpose flour
Thinly slivered green onion
   (optional)

Preheat oven to lowest setting. Line a baking sheet with parchment paper. Combine crab, 1 cup green onions and avocado in a large bowl. Mix eggs, salsa and salt; add to crab. Mix in breadcrumbs. Form mixture into 1 1/2-inch balls. Place on a prepared baking sheet. Cover with plastic and refrigerate 3 hours. (Can be prepared 1 day ahead and frozen. Do not thaw before cooking.) Line another baking sheet with paper towels. Pour oil into a large skillet to a depth of 3 inches. Heat to 350 degrees F. Dust fritters with flour. Carefully add to oil in batches (do not crowd) and cook until golden brown, about 2 minutes per side for refrigerated fritters and about 3 minutes per side for frozen. Drain on paper towels. Transfer to prepared sheet and keep warm in oven until all are cooked. Garnish with green onion slivers and serve immediately.

Crab and Mushroom Cheesecake

Makes 12 servings

1 cup fresh grated Parmesan cheese
1 cup panko breadcrumbs
1/2 cup unsalted, melted butter
2 tablespoons olive oil
1 cup chopped onion
1/2 cup chopped green bell peppers
1/2 cup chopped red bell peppers
4 cups chopped fresh mushrooms
1 teaspoon salt

1 teaspoon freshly ground
   black pepper
1-3/4 pounds softened cream cheese
4 eggs
1/2 cup heavy cream
1 cup grated smoked Gouda cheese
2-1/2 cups lump crabmeat
2 diced scallions

Preheat oven to 350 degrees F. Combine Parmesan cheese, breadcrumbs and butter until well blended. Press mixture into bottom of a 9-inch springform pan. In a skillet, sauté onion and bell peppers in oil over medium heat until onion is soft. Stir in mushrooms, salt and pepper and sauté 2 to 5 minutes. Remove from heat. With an electric mixer, beat the cream cheese and eggs until thick. Beat in the cream, Gouda cheese, sautéed vegetables and crabmeat. Mix for about 2 minutes. Pour into springform pan and bake 1 hour. Remove and cool. Sprinkle with scallions and serve.

Crab Dip

Makes 8 servings

1 cup mayonnaise
6 ounces cream cheese
6 tablespoons sour cream
1 tablespoon prepared horseradish
1 teaspoon lemon juice
1/4 cup grated Parmesan cheese

1/4 teaspoon white pepper
1-1/2 teaspoons hot sauce
1-1/2 teaspoons Worcestershire sauce
1-1/2 pounds crabmeat, picked over
   to remove shell

Preheat oven to 350 degrees F. In a large bowl, combine mayonnaise, cream cheese, sour cream, horseradish, lemon juice, Parmesan, pepper, hot sauce and Worcestershire sauce. If using a food processor, transfer mixture to a mixing bowl, and then add crabmeat. Mix well, being careful not to break up the crabmeat too finely. Transfer to a baking dish and bake until browned, about 20 minutes. Serve with toasted rounds of French bread.

Hot Crab Appetizers

Makes 10 servings

3 strips cooked and crumbled bacon
1 pound crabmeat
3 green onions chopped
1 teaspoon lemon juice
3/4 cup mayonnaise

1/2 cup shredded Cheddar cheese
1/4 cup chopped green or red bell
   pepper
Tabasco sauce to taste
English muffins

Mix all ingredients together. Lightly toast English muffins; then spread with crab mixture. Broil for 5 to 10 minutes. Cut into quarters and pass. Can also use toasted baguette slices.

Baked Crab, Brie and Artichoke Dip

Makes 6 to 8 servings

1 medium leek (white part only), finely chopped

1 medium sweet onion, finely chopped

1/2 cup drained finely chopped canned artichoke hearts

1/2 cup thawed frozen chopped spinach

1 pound Brie cheese

2 tablespoons minced garlic

2 tablespoons olive oil

1/4 cup medium dry white wine

2/3 cup heavy cream

3 tablespoons finely chopped fresh parsley leaves

2 tablespoons finely chopped fresh dill leaves

1 tablespoon finely chopped fresh tarragon leaves

1 pound fresh jumbo lump crabmeat

2 tablespoons Dijon mustard

1 teaspoon Tabasco sauce

Salt and pepper to taste

Preheat oven to 425 degrees F. Lightly oil shallow baking dish (about 6 cups volume). Trim and finely chop leek. In a large bowl of water, wash leek well and lift from water into a large sieve to drain. Finely chop onion. Rinse and finely chop artichoke hearts. Squeeze dry and finely chop spinach. Discard rind from Brie and cut into 1/4-inch pieces. In a heavy skillet, cook leek, onion and garlic in oil over moderate heat, stirring, until pale golden. Stir in artichoke hearts and spinach. Add wine and cook, stirring, 3 minutes. Add cream and simmer, stirring, 1 minute. Add Brie, stirring until it just begins to melt. Remove skillet from heat and stir herbs into mixture. Pick over crabmeat. In a large bowl, stir together crabmeat, mustard, Tabasco sauce, and salt and pepper to taste and stir in cheese mixture. Spread mixture evenly in baking dish and bake in the middle of oven 15 to 20 minutes, or until golden. Serve dip hot with toasts.

Belgian Endive with Lump Crab Salad

Makes 10 servings

1/2 pound jumbo lump crabmeat

2 tablespoons finely diced red bell pepper

2 tablespoons finely diced green bell pepper

2 tablespoons finely diced yellow pepper

1/4 cup finely diced red onion

1/4 cup chopped fresh cilantro

2 tablespoons fresh lime juice

Salt and pepper to taste

16 Belgian endive leaves

In a small mixing bowl, combine the crabmeat, peppers, onion, cilantro and lime juice. Season the crab mixture with salt and pepper to taste. Just before serving, spoon some of the crab salad into each of the Belgian endive leaves. Arrange on a platter and serve at once.

Herb Blini with Smoked Salmon and Horseradish Crème Fraîche

Makes 4 servings

3/4 cup instant oatmeal

3/4 cup all-purpose flour

Kosher salt

3/4 cup milk, warmed

1 tablespoon sugar

1 (1/4-ounce) envelope active
dry yeast

2 large egg whites, room
temperature

2 tablespoons chopped dill

1 tablespoon chopped Italian parsley

2 tablespoons chopped chives,
separated

2 teaspoons extra virgin olive oil,
separated

1/4 cup crème fraîche

2 tablespoons prepared horseradish

Freshly ground pepper

1/2 pound sliced smoked salmon

In a food processor, pulse the oatmeal to break it down a little. In a medium bowl, combine the ground oats with the flour and 1/2 teaspoon of salt. In a small bowl, mix the warm milk with the sugar and yeast. Add the milk mixture to the oatmeal mixture and stir well. Cover the bowl with plastic wrap and let stand in a warm place until the batter has doubled in volume, about 45 minutes. In a bowl, using an electric mixer, beat the egg whites at medium speed until soft peaks form. Fold a third of the egg whites into the oatmeal batter, and then fold in the remaining whites along with the dill, parsley and 1 tablespoon of the chives. In a large nonstick skillet, heat 1 teaspoon of the olive oil. Ladle 2 tablespoons of batter into the skillet for each blini, gently spreading them to 3-1/2-inch rounds. Cook over moderate heat until golden on both sides, about 6 minutes. Transfer the cooked blini to a warm platter and repeat with the remaining oil and batter. In a bowl, mix the crème fraîche with the horseradish; season with salt and pepper. Spoon some horseradish crème fraîche on each blini, top with smoked salmon and sprinkle with the remaining chives and some pepper. Serve immediately.

Salmon Spread

Makes 3 1/2 cups

1 (14-ounce) can red salmon, drained

8 ounces cream cheese

3 tablespoons finely chopped green
onions or red onion

2 tablespoons mayonnaise

2 tablespoons lemon juice

1/2 teaspoon salt

2 teaspoons Worcestershire sauce

1 garlic clove, pressed

Mix and serve with sliced dark cocktail bread.

Navajo Wedding, *1936, by Sybil Yazzie L., Navajo, #59383/13. Museum of Indian Arts and Culture/Laboratory of Anthropology, Department of Cultural Affairs, www.miaclab.org. Photo by Blair Clark.*

Smoked Trout Tartare

Makes 10 to 12 appetizers

4 ounces smoked trout, thinly sliced

2 tablespoons heavy cream

2 tablespoons fresh dill or fennel frond, snipped with scissors

Optional: Salmon can substitute trout in this recipe, if desired.

Trim any unwanted bits and ends from the fish. Lay each slice flat on a cutting board and cut into thin matchstick-size strips, keeping the strips evenly aligned. Cut crosswise into tiny cubes of fish about the size of the fat end of a pencil. (You want elegantly chunky tartare, not mashed.) Toss with the cream and dill.

Smoked Salmon Canapé

Makes 10 servings

2 tablespoons mayonnaise

1 tablespoon plus 1 teaspoon horseradish

1 tablespoon dill

2 tablespoons chopped onion

1 tablespoon chopped parsley

1 package hard bread rounds or toasted buttered bread cut in 4 pieces

2 to 3 sliced red apples

1 (6-ounce) can smoked salmon

Extra dill for garnish

Mix mayonnaise, horseradish, dill, onion and parsley. Spread the mixture over the bread rounds or toast. Layer 1 to 2 apple slices (depending on the size of the bread) over the mixture. Layer the smoked salmon over the apple. Garnish with the extra dill.

Southwest Fried Oysters

Makes 24 servings

2 pints fresh select oysters, drained

2 cups buttermilk

1 cup all-purpose flour

1/2 cup yellow cornmeal

1 tablespoon paprika

1-1/2 teaspoons garlic powder

1-1/2 teaspoons dried oregano

1-1/2 teaspoons chili powder

1-1/2 teaspoons ground red pepper

1/2 teaspoon dried mustard

1/2 teaspoon black pepper

Vegetable oil

Combine oysters and buttermilk in a large shallow dish or zip-top plastic freezer bag. Cover or seal and chill at least 2 hours. Drain oysters well. Combine flour and the next 8 ingredients. Dredge oysters in flour mixture, shaking off excess. Pour oil to a depth of 1 inch in a Dutch oven; heat to 370 degrees F. Fry oysters in batches, 3 minutes or until golden. Drain on paper towels. Serve with toothpicks and cocktail or tartar sauce.

Salmon Tartare

Makes 8 to 10 servings

2 pounds fresh salmon fillets
completely free of bones, skin
and fat
1 finely minced red onion
1/2 cup drained capers
1/2 cup chopped fresh mint

2 tablespoons vodka
1/4 cup extra virgin olive oil
Fresh lemon juice
Salt and freshly ground pepper to
taste

Cut the salmon into small pieces and put in a food processor until finely chopped. Do not puree. Combine all the ingredients in a bowl, cover and refrigerate until cold. Remove to serving dish and serve with rye bread or crackers.

Spicy salmon variation:
Combine 1/4 cup Dijon mustard, 1/3 cup pureed chipotle chile peppers canned in adobo sauce, 2/3 cup minced green onion, 1/2 cup drained capers, 1/4 cup olive oil and freshly ground black pepper to taste. Add 2 pounds salmon fillets completely free of bones, skin and fat. Finely dice salmon, add to mixture and serve immediately.

Smoked Salmon and Chive Mascarpone Mousse

Makes about 16 servings

1 teaspoon unflavored gelatin
3 tablespoons fresh lemon juice
1-1/2 cups mascarpone cheese
(about 3/4 pound)
3/4 cup sour cream, separated
2 peeled and quartered
hard-boiled eggs

2 tablespoons drained bottled
horseradish
1 teaspoon salt
Pepper to taste
6 ounces thinly sliced smoked
salmon
1/4 cup chopped fresh chives

Combine gelatin and lemon juice in a small saucepan and let stand 10 minutes. Beat together mascarpone and 1/2 cup sour cream. Force eggs through a coarse sieve into mascarpone mixture. Stir in horseradish, salt and pepper. Add remaining 1/4 cup sour cream to gelatin mixture and heat over moderately low heat, stirring, just until gelatin is dissolved. Add to mascarpone mixture and stir well. Line a 3-cup glass bowl or decorative mold with plastic wrap. Cut about a fourth of the salmon into 1-inch strips and line mold with strips, leaving a space between each and letting ends hang over. Chop remaining salmon and fold with chives into mascarpone mixture. Spoon into mold and fold ends of salmon strips over top. Chill mousse, covered, at least 2 hours, or until firm, and up to 2 days. Invert a platter over mold and using plastic wrap to pull it out, invert mousse onto platter. Remove plastic wrap. Serve with toast or crackers.

Salmon and Dill Quesadillas with Salmon Caviar

Makes 8 servings

6 (6-inch) flour tortillas
2 cups grated Monterey Jack
    cheese
2 cups grated white Cheddar
    cheese
4 tablespoons chopped red onion
5 tablespoons chopped fresh dill
Salt and ground pepper to taste

DILL SOUR CREAM

1 cup sour cream
2 tablespoons chopped fresh dill
Ground pepper to taste

GARNISH

16 thin slices smoked salmon
Dill Sour Cream
8 teaspoons salmon caviar

Preheat oven to 450 degrees F. Place 4 tortillas on an ungreased baking sheet. Sprinkle each with the two cheeses, onion and dill and season with salt and pepper. Stack 1 tortilla on top of the other so you have 2 stacks, and then top those with the other 2 tortillas. Bake 8 to 12 minutes until crisp and cheese has melted. Cut each tortilla into eighths. Garnish each with smoked salmon, Dill Sour Cream and salmon caviar and serve.

Oyster Shooters

Makes 6 servings

6 oysters, shucked
3 ribs celery
1 small bunch cilantro, washed
Sea salt to taste
1 cup spicy tomato puree

2 to 3 tablespoons
    horseradish
2 cups half-and-half

Refrigerate the oysters in their juice. Put the celery and cilantro through a juicer. Salt to taste and refrigerate. Put the tomato puree into a container and chill in the refrigerator. When you are ready to assemble them, put about 1 inch of tomato puree in the bottom of each glass. Add an oyster with a tad of the oyster juice and a teaspoon of celery-cilantro juice. Combine the horseradish and half-and-half and bring to a simmer. Whisk this mixture until frothy, then spoon onto the oysters and serve.

Spinach Oyster Dip

Makes 15 servings

4 packages frozen chopped spinach, cook as directed (save liquid) or 8 cooked finely chopped artichoke hearts

2 heaping tablespoons chopped onion

4 tablespoons butter

2 heaping tablespoons flour

1/2 cup evaporated milk

1/2 cup spinach liquid

1/2 teaspoon black pepper

3/4 teaspoon celery salt

6 ounces jalapeño cheese

1 teaspoon Worcestershire, Tabasco or red pepper sauce

1 pint oysters, drained and chopped

In a saucepan, sauté onion in butter until transparent. Add flour, milk and spinach liquid. Add seasoning, cheese, drained spinach, oysters and Worcestershire sauce. Simmer until oysters are done, about 30 minutes. If too thick, add a little spinach liquid. Can be made a day ahead and warmed in a double boiler. Put in a chafing dish to serve.

Smoked Scallop and Cucumber Appetizers

Makes 24 servings

HORSERADISH CREAM

1/2 cup crème fraîche

1/4 to 1/3 cup prepared horseradish, drained and squeezed

1 tablespoon whole grain mustard

1-1/4 tablespoons fresh lemon juice

1/2 teaspoon ground white pepper

2 tablespoons chopped chives

SCALLOP AND CUCUMBER APPETIZERS

1 English cucumber, diced into 24 half-inch pieces

12 to 16 ounces smoked bay scallops (about 50)

Horseradish Cream: Stir together the crème fraîche, horseradish, mustard, lemon juice, pepper and chopped chives in a bowl. Cover with plastic wrap and refrigerate for 4 hours or up to 48 hours.

Scallop and Cucumber Appetizers: Using a melon baller, scoop out the center of each cucumber slice to form a hollow. Mix together the scallops and the Horseradish Cream in a bowl until well coated. Spoon the scallop mixture onto the cucumber slices. Garnish each appetizer with a lemon slice and parsley sprig.

Chance Encounter, *n.d., by Walter Ufer, oil on canvas, 20 x 25 inches. Collection of the New Mexico Museum of Art, gift of the Museum of New Mexico Foundation in honor and memory of Mr. and Mrs. Lewis Barker, 1979. Photo by Blair Clark.*

Clam Puffs

Makes 8 servings

1 cup clam broth
1/2 cup butter
1 cup flour
4 eggs, room temperature

FILLING

3 (8-ounce) cans minced clams
6 (3-ounce) packages chive cream
  cheese
6 dashes Tabasco sauce
1/2 teaspoon pepper
1 teaspoon Lawry's Seasoned Salt

Preheat oven to 350 degrees F. Heat liquid in a saucepan. Add butter and bring to a boil. Add flour and stir with a wooden spoon until mixture leaves sides of pan and forms a soft ball. Transfer to a mixing bowl. Add 4 eggs, one at a time, beating thoroughly each time until thick dough is formed. Place level teaspoons of batter on ungreased baking sheet, 1 inch apart. Bake 10 minutes. Reduce heat to 250 degrees F without opening oven and bake for 15 to 20 minutes. Cool, cut in half and fill. Replace tops. If desired, you may freeze flat on a tray. When firm, pack in plastic bags or containers.

Drain clams. Soften cheese. Combine all ingredients and mix thoroughly. Fill puffs. Heat at 350 degrees for 10 to 15 minutes before serving.

Smoked Oyster Dip

Makes 6 to 8 servings

6 ounces cottage cheese
3 ounces softened cream cheese
3 teaspoons lemon juice
2 teaspoons Worcestershire sauce

2 (3-ounce) cans undrained, chopped
  smoked oysters
1/2 cup crushed potato chips
Salt and pepper to taste

Cream cottage cheese, cream cheese, lemon juice and Worcestershire sauce. Fold in the remaining ingredients, blend and refrigerate for 3 to 4 hours. Serve with crackers.

Hot Clam Dip

2 tablespoons minced onion

2 tablespoons butter

1 (7-1/2-ounce) can minced clams, drained

2 tablespoons ketchup

4 to 5 drops Tabasco sauce

1 cup diced or shredded old English cheese

3 tablespoons chopped ripe olives

1 teaspoon Worcestershire sauce

In a saucepan, sauté onion in butter 1 minute and add remaining ingredients. Heat until cheese melts and mixture is hot. Serve with crackers.

Lobster Tacos

Makes 10 servings

CHILE DE ARBOL SAUCE

1 tablespoon olive oil

1/4 onion finely chopped

2 tablespoons tomato paste

2 stemmed, dried chile de arbol chopped

1 chopped garlic clove

1-1/2 cups whipping cream

1 tablespoon finely chopped fresh cilantro

BLACK BEAN PUREE

3 cups water

1 cup dried black beans

1/2 onion chopped

Salt to taste

TACOS

1-1/2 tablespoons butter

2 pounds thawed frozen lobster tails, shelled and cut in 1/4-inch cubes

Salt and pepper to taste

10 (6-inch) flour tortillas, each cut into 4-inch rounds

1 pitted, peeled avocado, cut lengthwise into thin slices

Fresh chopped cilantro

Chile De Arbol Sauce: Heat oil in a skillet over medium heat. Add onion, tomato paste, chile and garlic. Sauté until onion is soft. Add cream. Stir and simmer until sauce consistency. Transfer to small bowl and blend in cilantro. This can be made ahead. Cover and chill. When ready to make tacos, it can be heated.

Black Bean Puree: Bring all ingredients to a boil in a saucepan. Lower heat to medium low, cover and simmer until tender. Place in a blender and puree until smooth. Add salt to taste. Cover and chill if made ahead. It can be heated in the microwave when preparing the tacos.

Tacos: Melt butter in a skillet over medium heat. Add lobster and sauté about 3 to 4 minutes. Salt and pepper to taste and set lobster aside. Cook tortillas in a dry skillet over medium heat until lightly toasted, about 1 minute on each side. Place tortillas on a platter. Spread each with a heaping teaspoon of Black Bean Puree. Put lobster pieces on tortillas and drizzle with Chile de Arbol Sauce. Top each with an avocado slice, sprinkle with cilantro and serve.

Chili and Corn-Crusted Calamari with Tangy Citrus Aioli

Makes 6 servings

TANGY CITRUS AIOLI

Juice of 1 lemon (mince and reserve zest)

1/4 cup fresh orange juice

1/2 jalapeño seeded and minced

1 tablespoon minced garlic

1 cup mayonnaise

1/2 teaspoon nam pla (Thai fish sauce)

Finely minced zest of 1 lime

Finely minced zest of 1 orange

CALAMARI

1/2 cup yellow cornmeal

1/4 cup chili powder

2 tablespoons all-purpose flour

Peanut oil

1 pound cleaned squid, mantles cut into 1/4-inch rings and tentacles into bite-size pieces

Combine the lemon juice, orange juice, jalapeño and garlic in a small nonreactive saucepan set over high heat. Bring to a boil and cook until the juice is very syrupy and reduced to about 3 tablespoons, about 10 minutes. Spoon the citrus reduction into a small bowl and let cool to room temperature. Stir in the mayonnaise, nam pla and all of the minced citrus zest. Mix well; the aioli should be tart and tangy. If it tastes too sweet, add a squeeze of juice from the zested lime. If you want more spiciness, add the remaining half jalapeño. This can be made ahead and kept refrigerated for up to 2 days. Serve chilled.

Sift together the cornmeal, chili powder and flour in a small bowl. Heat 2 inches of peanut oil to 350 degrees F in a deep fryer or heavy-bottomed saucepan. Toss the calamari (squid) in the cornmeal mixture and remove with tongs or a slotted spoon. When the oil is hot, carefully add half of the coated squid and fry until golden brown, about 1 minute. Remove with tongs or a slotted spoon and drain on paper towels. Repeat with the remaining squid. To serve, pile on a large platter and serve citrus aioli for dipping.

Meat Appetizers

Three Bears, 1936, Quincey Tahoma, Navajo, #51437/13. Museum of Indian Arts and Culture/Laboratory of Anthropology, Department of Cultural Affairs, www.miaclab.org. Photo by Blair Clark.

Tasty Egg Rolls

Makes 8 to 12 servings

2 pounds spicy ground pork sausage

3 tablespoons grated fresh ginger

5 cloves garlic, pressed

2 (10-ounce) bags shredded coleslaw mix

2 (16-ounce) packages egg roll wrappers

Canola oil

SPICY SAUCE

6 tablespoons soy sauce

6 tablespoons white vinegar

2 tablespoons sugar

4 tablespoons dry sherry

1 teaspoon cornstarch

7 tablespoons chicken broth

6 tablespoons sesame oil

3 cloves garlic, minced

1 teaspoon diced fresh ginger

2 green onions trimmed and diced

1/2 teaspoon ground Szechuan peppercorns

2 tablespoons chile paste

2 tablespoons chopped fresh cilantro

In a large skillet, cook the sausage over medium heat. Stir until it crumbles and is no longer pink. Drain off fat. Stir in ginger and garlic and cook for two minutes. Add coleslaw and cook until slaw is tender, stirring occasionally. Remove skillet from heat and let cool for at least 40 minutes. Spoon 1/4 cup of mixture onto the center of each egg roll wrapper. Fold three corners of each wrapper over filling, one at a time. Lightly brush remaining corner with water. Tightly roll filled portion toward the remaining corner and press to seal. In a deep skillet, pour canola oil to a depth of about 2 inches. Heat to 375 degrees F and fry in batches until golden brown (turning once). Drain on paper towels and serve while hot with Spicy Sauce for dipping.

Combine first 6 ingredients and whisk well. In a skillet, warm the sesame oil over medium heat and add the garlic, ginger, onions, peppercorns and chile paste. Stir briefly and remove from heat. Add the soy mixture, and then the cilantro. Serve in two small bowls for dipping.

Asian Barbecued Ribs

Makes 8 servings

2 pounds baby back ribs

Salt and freshly ground black pepper

2 tablespoons minced fresh ginger

1 tablespoon minced garlic

2 green onions thinly sliced

1/2 cup hoisin sauce

1/4 cup oyster sauce

1/3 cup ketchup

1 tablespoon soy sauce

2 teaspoons hot chile paste

1/4 cup packed light brown sugar

1 teaspoon sesame oil

1/4 cup rice wine vinegar

Preheat oven to 375 degrees F. Fit a roasting pan with a flat rack. Sprinkle both sides of the ribs with salt and pepper. Place on the rack in the pan. Bake for 45 minutes. Meanwhile, combine the remaining ingredients in a food processor. Process until smooth, about 30 seconds. Transfer the glaze to a bowl, or cover and refrigerate for up to 1 week. Remove the ribs from the oven; leave the oven on. When they are cool enough to handle, slice the racks into individual ribs. Toss the ribs in the prepared glaze, coating well. Place the ribs on a baking sheet and bake until the glaze caramelizes and the ribs are tender, 20 to 30 minutes more. Serve with small plates.

Mustard and Honey Spareribs

Makes 12 to 16 servings

1 tablespoon dry mustard

1 teaspoon sage

1 tablespoon salt

10 pounds spareribs, cut into 2-inch pieces

1 (12-ounce) bottle beer or ale

1 cup honey

4 peeled and minced shallots

3 stemmed, seeded and minced serrano chiles

1 tablespoon lemon juice

Preheat oven to 350 degrees F. Mix all the spices and rub on the ribs. Mix the beer, honey, shallots, chiles and lemon juice and then pour mixture over the ribs. Marinate overnight. Roast uncovered for 2 hours. Serve hot with plenty of napkins.

Pork and Currant Rolls

Makes 12 rolls

3 tablespoons peanut oil, separated

1-1/2 cups finely chopped onion

2 pounds ground pork

Salt and freshly ground pepper to taste

1/2 cup toasted sliced almonds

1/2 cup toasted pine nuts

1/2 cup dried currants

2 tablespoons chopped parsley

6 sheets filo pastry

Preheat oven to 425 degrees F. Heat 1 tablespoon of the oil in a nonstick frying pan over medium heat. Add onions and fry, stirring, until golden, about 5 to 7 minutes. Add the pork and 1 tablespoon of the oil to the pan and cook, breaking up the pork until lightly browned, 3 to 4 minutes. Season to taste with salt and pepper. Transfer pork mixture to a bowl and add the remaining ingredients, except pastry, and mix. Cut filo sheets in half crosswise. Place a half sheet on a work surface; cover remaining sheets with a damp towel. On half of the sheet, spread 1/12 of the pork mixture in a rectangle 3 inches long by 3/4 inch wide, leaving the bottom edge and sides uncovered. Fold the bottom edge over the mixture, and then fold in the sides and roll up the pastry. You should have a triangle-shaped pastry roll. Using a pastry brush, oil a baking sheet with the remaining 1 tablespoon of oil. Arrange rolls on the sheet 1/2 inch apart and lightly brush each pastry with some oil. Bake until golden and crisp, about 20 to 25 minutes, and then serve.

Ham Appetizer

Makes 16 servings

6 eggs
1/4 cup butter
1/4 cup cracker crumbs
1 cup sour cream

1/2 cup grated Swiss cheese
2 cups minced cooked ham
2 teaspoons caraway seeds

Preheat oven to 375 degrees F. In a large bowl, beat eggs until light and thick. Add the rest of the ingredients and mix. Pour into a greased 9 x 9-inch casserole dish and bake until brown, about 15 minutes. Cut into squares and serve.

Ham Balls

Makes 120 balls

1 pound ground ham
1 pound ground steak
1 pound pork
2 cups soft breadcrumbs
1 cup milk
2 eggs

SAUCE FOR HAM BALLS

2 cups brown sugar
1 cup vinegar
2 teaspoons dry mustard
1 cup water

Mix all ingredients for balls together. Form into balls the size of a walnut. Drop meatballs into sauce and cook slowly for 1 hour. Serve with Sauce for Ham Balls.

Cook all sauce ingredients in a saucepan until bubbly. These freeze well.

Picadillo Dip

Makes 12 servings

1/2 pound spicy sausage
1 pound lean ground beef
1 teaspoon salt
1/4 teaspoon ground black pepper
1 (16-ounce) can diced tomatoes
4 chopped green onions
2 tablespoons drained capers
1/2 cup almond slices

1 clove garlic, diced
1 (6-ounce) can tomato paste
2 jalapeños, seeded and diced
1/2 cup golden raisins
1/4 teaspoon oregano
1/2 cup sliced pimiento-stuffed
   green olives

In a large bowl, mix the meats together by hand. Pour water over meat to barely cover. Add salt and pepper and stir meat until well blended. Remove to a skillet and simmer, covered, for 30 minutes. Add remaining ingredients and cook 30 minutes. Serve hot in a chafing dish with chips.

The Rendezvous, *1950, by E. Martin Hennings. Collection of the New Mexico Museum of Art. Photo by Blair Clark.*

Steak with Scotch Sauce

Makes 8 servings

3 pounds New York strip steak, cut
    in bite-size cubes
Kosher salt
Ground green peppercorns
1/2 cup butter, divided

1 cup scotch
1 cup canned beef broth
2 teaspoons dry tarragon
1 tablespoon arrowroot

Season the steak with salt and green peppercorns. Melt 3 tablespoons butter in a pan over high heat. Add steak and sear for 3 minutes. Turn and sear other side for 3 minutes. Reduce heat to medium high and sauté for 10 minutes on each side. Remove steak to cutting board. Add and melt remaining butter; then add scotch and reduce to a glaze. Add beef broth and tarragon; cook 2 minutes. Stir arrowroot into sauce in a chafing dish. Return steak cubes to the chafing dish. Serve with toothpicks.

Marinated Flank Steak and Horseradish Sauce

Makes 6 to 8 servings

HORSERADISH
SAUCE

1/2 cup sour cream
1 tablespoon plus 1 teaspoon finely
    chopped horseradish
2 green onions, finely chopped

STEAK

1/2 cup soy sauce
1/2 cup white wine
1/2 cup chopped onion
2 tablespoons chopped
    fresh rosemary
2 tablespoons olive oil
2 garlic cloves, chopped
2 pounds flank steak

Horseradish Sauce: Combine all sauce ingredients in a bowl and mix well. Chill, covered, until serving time.

Steak: Combine the soy sauce, wine, onion, rosemary, olive oil and garlic in a bowl and mix well. Pour over the steak in a shallow dish, turning to coat. Marinate, covered, in the refrigerator for 8 to 10 hours, turning occasionally. Drain the steak, reserving the marinade. Grill the steak over hot coals or under a broiler for 6 minutes per side for rare, basting occasionally, if desired, with the reserved marinade. Remove the steak to a serving platter. Let stand for 15 minutes. Slice thinly across the grain and serve with Horseradish Sauce and small sliced buns.

Sauerkraut Meatballs

Makes 8 servings

1/2 pound sausage meat
1/2 pound buffalo ground round
1 cup diced onion
1 (16-ounce) can drained and finely
    chopped sauerkraut
3 tablespoons panko breadcrumbs
1 (6-ounce) package softened cream
    cheese
4 tablespoons parsley

2 teaspoons prepared mustard
3 garlic cloves, minced
1/2 teaspoon freshly ground
    black pepper
1/2 cup all-purpose flour
3 beaten eggs
1/2 cup milk
2 cups breadcrumbs

Preheat oven to 350 degrees F. In a skillet, sauté meats and onion until meats are brown. Pour off the fat. Add sauerkraut and panko breadcrumbs. In a mixing bowl, combine cream cheese, parsley, mustard, garlic and pepper. Blend into meat mixture. Shape mixture into 1-inch balls and coat each with flour. Combine the eggs and milk. Dip the balls into the milk-and-egg mixture. Finally, roll them in the breadcrumbs. Heat the meatballs in the oven for 30 minutes, and then serve.

Savory Oriental Lamb Chops

Makes 4 to 8 servings

4 tablespoons dark sesame oil
12 to 16 tiny lamb riblets,
    trimmed of fat
1 cup finely chopped yellow onion
4 cloves garlic, minced

4 tablespoons soy sauce
4 tablespoons oriental chile paste
1 cup orange marmalade
2 tablespoons rice wine vinegar
1-1/2 tablespoons minced
    fresh gingerroot

Heat oil in a large enough skillet to hold all the lamb chops. Add the chops and brown lightly on both sides. Remove from skillet to paper towels to drain. Add the onion and garlic to the skillet. Cover and cook over low heat for about 20 minutes, or until tender. Add the rest of the ingredients and simmer for 3 minutes, stirring constantly. Return chops to skillet. Cover and cook over low heat for about 8 minutes. Turn once. Serve immediately with plenty of napkins.

Savory Chicken Wings

Makes 8 servings

1/4 cup soy sauce
1 tablespoon honey
1 tablespoon Dijon mustard
1 clove garlic, crushed

1/4 teaspoon hot pepper sauce
2 tablespoons tequila
2 pounds chicken wings, cut in half

Preheat oven to 375 degrees F. Mix all ingredients except wings; add wings and marinate in refrigerator overnight. Drain wings. Arrange in single layer on a baking pan. Bake for 20 minutes. Serve hot or cold.

Variation: Simmer wings in soy mixture for 1 hour, stirring often. Drain and serve.

Navajo Rug, 1900–1920, #16032/12. Museum of Indian Arts and Culture/Laboratory of Anthropology, Department of Cultural Affairs, www.mia-clab.org. Photo by Blair Clark.

Meatballs in Chutney Sauce

Makes 20 servings

2 pounds lean ground round
1 pound ground Italian or spice
    sausage
All-purpose flour
1-1/4 cups sour cream

1 (8-ounce) jar of mango
    or peach chutney
3/4 cup dry sherry
Freshly ground pepper

Combine meats and roll into 1-inch balls. Roll each in flour to lightly dust. Sauté meatballs in a skillet over medium heat until done. Drain. Combine other ingredients in a saucepan over medium heat and stir until well blended. Add meatballs and heat until they have absorbed some of the juices. Serve in a chafing dish to keep hot.

Chipotle Sauce for Meatballs

Makes 5 cups

1-1/2 pounds Roma tomatoes
6 to 10 chipotle chiles in
    adobo sauce
1/4 cup chopped shallots
4 to 5 tablespoons canola oil
1 cup beef stock

Salt and pepper
1/4 cup diced garlic
1/2 teaspoon cumin

(Note: Buy frozen meatballs
    or prepare your own.)

Place tomatoes in a large bowl and cover with boiling water. Let stand for at least 6 minutes. Remove from water and peel. In a blender, mix tomatoes, chiles and shallots until smooth. Over medium heat, heat oil in a Dutch oven, then add the tomato mixture. Cook and stir for about 7 minutes. Add the stock and seasonings and simmer for 5 minutes. To cook meatballs, add them to the sauce, cover and cook over low heat until done.

Barbecue Venison

Makes 16 to 20 servings

1/4 cup vinegar
1/8 cup brown sugar
1 (3-pound) venison roast
1 large onion, diced
1-1/2 cups chopped celery
1 cup ketchup
3 tablespoons Worcestershire sauce

1 teaspoon chili powder
1-1/2 cups water
4 tablespoons liquid smoke
Salt and pepper
1/4 teaspoon oregano
2 bay leaves
2 garlic cloves, crushed

Preheat oven to 275 degrees F. Mix vinegar and brown sugar. In a roaster, marinate meat in vinegar and brown sugar for 30 minutes. Mix remaining ingredients and pour over meat. Tightly cover and bake for 5 to 6 hours, or until meat will shred. Serve on hot buttered cocktail-size rolls.

City Different Beef Dip

Makes 8 servings

1 (8-ounce) package cream cheese
2 tablespoons milk
1 (2-1/2-ounce) jar diced dried beef
1/4 cup chopped green bell pepper
1/4 teaspoon garlic powder
1/4 teaspoon pepper
1 tablespoon grated onion
1/2 cup sour cream
4 tablespoons grated onion

TOPPING

1/4 cup chopped pecans
1/4 teaspoon salt
2 tablespoons butter

Combine first nine ingredients and mix until well blended. Put into an 8-inch pie pan or ovenproof dish of the same capacity. Sauté pecans and salt in butter until nuts are lightly browned. Sprinkle over cheese-beef mixture. Bake for 20 minutes at 350 degrees F. Serve hot with low-salt crackers or Melba toast.

Teriyaki Beef Nuggets

Makes 24 pieces

1/2 cup soy sauce
2 tablespoons honey
1/4 teaspoon ground ginger
1 clove garlic, crushed
1 teaspoon grated onion
1/4 cup dry white wine

3/4 pound boneless top sirloin, cut
    into 1/2-inch diagonal slices
1 (6-ounce) can water chestnuts,
    halved

In a shallow bowl, combine soy sauce, honey, ginger, garlic, onion and wine. Wrap 1 slice of meat around each water chestnut half and secure with a toothpick. Marinate beef nuggets in soy sauce mixture for 1 hour. Place nuggets in a broiler pan and broil for 3 to 4 minutes on rack, 5 to 8 inches from heat, turning once or twice. Serve immediately.

Indian Chicken Balls

Makes 36 balls

1/2 pound cream cheese
2 tablespoons mayonnaise
1 cup chopped, cooked chicken
1 cup chopped, blanched almonds

1 tablespoon chopped chutney
1/2 teaspoon salt
1 tablespoon curry powder
2 cups Angel Flake coconut

Beat together cream cheese and mayonnaise. Add chicken, almonds, chutney, salt and curry powder. Shape into walnut-size balls and roll in coconut. Chill.

Eastern Lamb Kebabs

Makes 18 servings

3 pounds lamb shoulder or rump,
   boned, and cut in 1/2 x 2-inch
   slices
1 medium chopped onion
1 cup yogurt
1 teaspoon salt
1/2 teaspoon freshly ground pepper
Pinch finely ground sumac

ALTERNATE
MARINADE
FOR LAMB

1/2 cup olive oil
1/4 cup lime juice
1 teaspoon dry mustard
1/4 teaspoon thyme
1/8 teaspoon basil
1/8 teaspoon rosemary
1 bay leaf
Salt and freshly ground pepper
1 medium onion
Minced garlic

Flatten lamb pieces slightly on both sides. In a deep dish, mix onion, yogurt, salt, pepper and sumac, and then add the meat. Marinate meat for 2 days in the refrigerator. Remove and run small skewers through each piece of meat lengthwise. Place kebabs on a rack 3 inches from heat in preheated broiler. Broil 20 minutes, turning once. Serve hot.

Curried Beef Pasties

Makes 25 pieces

PASTIE

1 tablespoon butter
1/4 pound ground beef
6 chopped green onions, including
   tops
1/2 clove garlic, minced
1/4 teaspoon ground ginger
1/8 teaspoon ground cinnamon
1 teaspoon fresh lemon juice
1 teaspoon curry powder
1/2 teaspoon salt

DOUGH

1/4 cup softened butter
1 (3-ounce) package cream cheese
1/2 cup sifted all-purpose flour

Preheat oven to 350 degrees F. Blend all ingredients for pasties in a bowl and set aside. Cream together the butter and cheese. Add flour. Chill the dough. Roll the dough on a floured board to 1/8-inch thickness, or as thin as possible. Cut into 2-inch squares or circles. Place 1 teaspoon filling on half of each piece. Wet edges and fold remaining half over. Press edges together. Bake 20 minutes and serve.

Won Ton Chicken Bites

Makes 36 won tons

36 won ton wrappers
1/2 (16-ounce) bag coleslaw
1 cup chopped cooked chicken
1 (8-ounce) can finely chopped water
   chestnuts

5 thinly sliced green onions
2 teaspoons roasted sesame oil
4 tablespoons Chinese plum sauce

Preheat oven to 350 degrees F. Cut a 1/2-inch strip off one side of each won ton skin; pleat wrappers into oiled mini-muffin tins to make cups. Bake until golden, 8 minutes. Let stand at least 5 minutes. Place coleslaw, chicken, water chestnuts and green onions in a large bowl and stir in the sesame oil and plum sauce. Spoon the filling into the cooled won ton cups.

Bacon-Wrapped Duck Breast Hors d'oeuvres

Makes 8 to 10 servings

2 cups dry red wine
2 teaspoons garlic powder
1 tablespoon soy sauce
Salt and freshly ground black pepper
4 to 6 duck breasts, boned, skinned
   and cut into bite-size pieces
1/2 pound thinly sliced bacon strips,
   cut in half

PLUM SAUCE

4 tablespoons unsalted butter
1/4 cup firmly packed light brown
   sugar
1 tablespoon cognac
1 (10-ounce) jar red plum jelly

In a large bowl, combine red wine, garlic powder, soy sauce, salt and pepper. Add duck pieces and marinate, refrigerated, for 24 hours. Remove duck pieces from marinade and wrap 1/2 slice of bacon around each piece. Secure with wooden skewers. Can be prepared ahead to this point, covered and refrigerated. Roast at 350 degrees F for 25 to 30 minutes. Serve with Plum Sauce for dipping.

In a small saucepan, melt butter. Add brown sugar, cognac and jelly. Mix well and heat until bubbly. This recipe works with wild goose, dove, quail or pheasant.

Photo by Peter Vitale

Barbeque Wings

Makes 9 servings

18 whole chicken wings (about 3 pounds)

4 tablespoons lemon juice

2 tablespoons vegetable oil

2 tablespoons Worcestershire sauce

4 teaspoons Tabasco sauce

1 cup blue cheese dressing (use a good quality)

12 to 16 celery sticks

Halve wings. In a small dish, combine lemon juice, oil, Worcestershire sauce and Tabasco sauce. Reserve half of sauce in a separate bowl. Place wings in shallow dish and pour remaining sauce over them. Toss the wings to coat completely with sauce. Let stand 30 minutes. Prepare a hot fire. Grill the wings, turning often and brushing with reserved sauce (do not use sauce in which chicken marinated), 14 to 18 minutes, or until skin is browned and crisp and chicken is no longer pink near the bone. Serve on a large platter with blue cheese dressing and celery sticks.

Cumin-Coconut Chicken Skewers

Makes 15 servings

2 cloves garlic, minced

2-1/2 tablespoons ground cumin

1-1/2 tablespoons chili powder

1 tablespoon ground coriander

1-1/2 teaspoons paprika

1 cup coconut milk

2 teaspoons light brown sugar

3/4 teaspoon salt

3 (8-ounce) boneless, skinless chicken breasts

30 (6- to 8-inch) wooden skewers soaked in water 1 hour

2 tablespoons vegetable oil

Cracked black pepper for garnish

Combine the garlic, cumin, chili powder, coriander, paprika, coconut milk, brown sugar and salt in a bowl. Slice each chicken breast into 10 pieces by first cutting in half horizontally, then cutting each half into 5 strips. Thread each strip of chicken onto a skewer, place the skewers in a shallow baking dish and pour the marinade over them. Cool and put in refrigerator for 6 hours or overnight. In a large skillet, heat the oil and pan-sear the chicken skewers for 4 to 6 minutes on each side, until cooked through. Or bake them at 400 degrees F on a greased baking sheet for 10 to 12 minutes. Sprinkle with cracked pepper and serve.

Southwestern Appetizers

Sunflowers, 1937, Jose J. Garcia, Santo Domingo Pueblo, #51368/13. Museum of Indian Arts and Culture/Laboratory of Anthropology, Department of Cultural Affairs, www.miaclab.org. Photo by Blair Clark.

Appetizer Chiles Rellenos

Makes 16 squares

2 (4-ounce) cans whole green chiles

3 cups shredded Monterey Jack cheese

1-1/2 cups shredded sharp Cheddar cheese

2 eggs

2 tablespoons milk

1 tablespoon flour

Preheat oven to 350 degrees F. Cut chiles into thin strips. In a lightly greased 9-inch square pan, layer cheeses and chile strips, beginning and ending with cheeses. In a bowl, beat together eggs, milk and flour. Pour over layered ingredients. Bake for 45 minutes to 1 hour, or until firm. Cut into small squares and serve warm.

Jalapeño Cheese Balls

Makes about 36 servings

4-1/2- to 5-pound pork loin roast

2 teaspoons salt

1 medium onion, chopped

4 cloves garlic, chopped

10 jalapeños, seeded and diced

1 (14-ounce) square Monterey Jack or Cheddar cheese

5 to 6 eggs

1/4 cup milk

2 cans plain breadcrumbs

Vegetable oil

Cook roast on stove with enough water to more than cover, adding salt, onion and garlic. Cook until fork tender. Cool and cut into small pieces. Put through a food processor until completely processed. Meat should be like soft dough. If meat feels dry, add a little broth. Add jalapeños to meat and mix thoroughly. Cut cheese into 1/3-inch squares. Wrap meat around cheese to form balls about 3/4 to 1 inch in diameter. Beat eggs and milk together. Place breadcrumbs in a large, flat dish. Dip chile balls into egg mixture; roll in the breadcrumbs. Repeat process. Heat oil in a skillet and immerse some of the chile balls in hot oil. Fry until chile balls are golden brown. Serve with toothpicks. For more spice, you can serve with salsa for dipping. These can be frozen and then heated for serving. This recipe can be made with ground beef instead of pork.

Tesuque Tortillas

Makes 12 pieces

3 whole wheat flour tortillas

1-1/2 cups grated Cheddar cheese (or laurel or clavel)

1-1/2 cups green chile sauce

Preheat oven to 350 degrees F. Cut each tortilla into 4 wedges. Place wedges together on a cookie sheet and spoon green chile sauce on the wedges. Spread the cheese on top. Bake until cheese is melted and starting to bubble. Transfer to a plate and serve hot.

Spicy Chicken Nachos

Makes 20 servings

3 cups skinned chicken breast, poached and diced

12 ounces cream cheese, softened

3 jalapeños, seeded and minced

1/2 cup minced green onions

2 cloves garlic, minced

1 teaspoon cumin

1-1/2 teaspoons chili powder

2 cups Monterey Jack cheese, grated

Salt and freshly ground black pepper to taste

1 package tostado rounds

Preheat oven to 375 degrees F. Combine all ingredients, except salt and pepper and chips, in a large bowl and mix thoroughly. Season with salt and pepper. Place a generous amount of chicken mixture on tostados. Place on a cookie sheet and bake until melting, about 5 to 8 minutes. Serve while hot.

Southwest Tomatillo Duck Triangles

Makes 24–32 triangles

8 (6-inch) flour tortillas, quartered

1-1/4 cups chopped tomatillos

1-1/4 cups chopped plum tomatoes

4 jalapeños, seeded and minced

3 tablespoons minced cilantro

2 tablespoons minced parsley

3 tablespoons fresh lime juice

2 cloves garlic, crushed

3/4 teaspoon Tabasco Sauce

1 teaspoon ground cumin

1 pound shredded white Cheddar cheese

1/2 teaspoon salt

1/2 teaspoon pepper

4 cups roast half duck (Maple Leaf Farms), follow package directions to prepare

1 cup thinly sliced red onion

Preheat oven to 375 degrees F. Place tortillas on a cookie sheet. Bake 5 to 7 minutes until lightly toasted. In a medium bowl, mix all ingredients, except the duck and onion. For each appetizer spread some of the tomatillo mixture on each tortilla quarter. Top with duck meat and some onion slices. Bake 10 to 15 minutes, until cheese is melted.

Empanaditas

Makes about 4 dozen

MEAT FILLING

2 cups ground or finely diced meat
   (pork or beef)
1 cup sugar
1-1/2 cups applesauce
1 teaspoon salt
1/2 teaspoon cinnamon
1/2 teaspoon allspice
1 teaspoon nutmeg
1 tablespoon vanilla
1 cup diced cranberries
1 cup roasted, shelled pine nuts
2 tablespoons blackberry brandy
1 cup mincemeat or raisins (optional)

PASTRY

4 cups flour
1/2 teaspoon salt
2 teaspoons baking powder
3 tablespoons sugar
3/4 cup shortening (part lard)
1/2 cup milk
Water, as needed

Cover meat with water in a large kettle and simmer until tender, about 1 hour. Cool. Grind meat in a grinder and place in a large bowl. Add remaining ingredients for meat filling. Mix well with hands, using applesauce (or meat stock) to moisten. Let mixture stand while preparing pastry.

Sift flour into a large bowl and add salt, baking powder and sugar. Cut in shortening. Mix in milk and water to form soft dough. Knead dough with hands for about 3 minutes. Form dough into balls about 1-1/2 inches in diameter. Roll out on a floured board. Place 2 teaspoons filling on half circle of dough, folding over other half circle to enclose. Pinch edges of dough together to prevent filling from leaking. Brush with egg whites. Bake at 350 degrees F on a greased cookie sheet until golden brown, about 15 minutes.

Tortilla Roll-Ups

Makes 48 roll-ups

3 (8-ounce) packages cream cheese
1 (8-ounce) container sour cream
2 tablespoons salsa
1/2 cup chopped onion
1 jalapeño, seeded and chopped
Juice from 1 lime
1/2 teaspoon salt
12 flour tortillas

Mix first 7 ingredients. Spread mixture on tortillas and roll. Cut each tortilla into quarters. Store in a plastic zipper bag in the refrigerator. Serve with salsa and guacamole.

Photo by Peter Vitale

Mexican Pizza

Makes 20 servings

1 (15-ounce) can tomato sauce

1 large yellow onion, chopped

1 (6-ounce) can chopped green chile

1/3 cup Romano cheese, grated

1 (4-ounce) package hard salami, cut into small bits

1 (8-ounce) package grated Cheddar cheese

1 package small tostados

Preheat oven to 350 degrees F. Put tomato sauce and onions in a saucepan and bring to a boil until thickened. Add green chile. Stir constantly. Add Romano cheese and remove from heat. Add salami to paste mixture. Put Cheddar cheese on top of each tostado. Then add a heaping tablespoon of the meat and tomato paste on top of cheese. Place on a cookie sheet and heat until the cheese melts.

Layered Rancher's Dip

Makes 11 cups

2 (8-1/2-ounce) cans jalapeño bean dip

2/3 cup sour cream

1 (1.25-ounce) package taco seasoning

2 (4-ounce) cans chopped green chiles

4 medium avocados, mashed with 2 tablespoons lime juice, 2 teaspoons salt and 1/4 teaspoon garlic powder mixed together

1 (8-ounce) package shredded Cheddar cheese

2 cups sliced green onions

2 cups chopped tomatoes

6 ounces sliced pitted ripe olives

Layer in order listed on a 10 x 15-inch platter. Serve with corn chips or Doritos.

Green Chile Con Queso

Makes 4 to 6 cups

1 medium onion, finely diced

2 cloves garlic, minced

2 tablespoons fat

2 tablespoons flour

1 cup chopped green chiles

1 medium tomato, chopped

1 cup evaporated milk

1/2 cup grated clavel cheese (found in Mexican markets)

1/2 cup Cheddar cheese, grated

1 pound processed cheese, grated

Combine onion, garlic and fat in top portion of double boiler. Cook at medium heat until onion is transparent. Add flour and stir. Add green chiles and tomato and bring to a boil. Remove from heat and add milk and cheeses. Place over boiling water and cook, stirring constantly, until cheeses are melted. Reduce heat and let simmer 1/2 hour. Serve with tostados.

Variations: Add 1/4 cup chopped pimentos, or add 1/4 cup diced jalapeños for stronger flavor.

Jicama with a Kick

Makes about 12 pieces

1 medium jicama
1/2 cup fresh lime juice

2 tablespoons Lawry's Seasoned
    Salt
2 tablespoons chili powder

Peel and cut jicama into strips, about finger size. Do not prepare in advance, as it dries out. In one bowl, put the lime juice, and in another bowl, mix chili powder and seasoned salt. Dip jicama in the lime juice, then in salt and chili powder.

Vaquero Salsa

Makes 4 to 5 cups

1/2 cup diced red bell pepper
1/2 cup sliced black olives
1/4 cup sliced green onions
1 (15-ounce) can black-eyed peas,
    drained and rinsed
1 (8-ounce) can shoe-peg corn,
    drained
4 tablespoons cilantro pesto

2 tablespoons red wine vinegar
Dash hot sauce (or 2 to 3 if you like
    it hot!)
Salt and ground black pepper
    to taste
Tortilla chips and pita wedges,
    for serving

Mix together red bell pepper, black olives, green onions, black-eyed peas and shoe-peg corn. In a small bowl, mix together cilantro pesto, red wine vinegar and hot sauce. Toss pesto mixture with black-eyed pea mixture. Salt and pepper to taste. Cover and chill until ready to serve. Serve with tortilla chips, pita wedges, or as a relish alongside grilled meat.

Mexican Mushrooms

Makes 16 servings

1/2 cup sharp Cheddar cheese
3/4 cup Monterey Jack cheese
1/4 to 1/3 cup sour cream
4 tablespoons sliced green onions
3 tablespoons chopped cilantro or
    parsley, or a mixture of both

4 tablespoons diced canned
    green chiles
1/3 cup butter
1-1/2 cloves garlic, pressed
16 (2-inch) fresh mushroom caps
Grated fresh Parmesan cheese

In a mixing bowl, toss Cheddar and Monterey Jack cheeses, sour cream, green onions, cilantro or parsley and chiles and set aside. In a saucepan, combine butter and garlic; warm to melt butter. Brush mushroom caps with the garlic butter and fill each cap with 1 generous tablespoon of the cheese mixture. Sprinkle generously with Parmesan cheese and broil until bubbly, about 3 to 5 minutes.

Pottery Maker, 1934, by Will Shuster, fresco, 47 x 23 inches. Collections of the New Mexico Museum of Art, on long-term loan from the U.S. General Services Administration, Public Works of Art Project, 1934. Photo by Blair Clark.

Corn Dip

Makes 20 servings

2 (15-ounce) cans whole-kernel
    corn, drained
2 (4-ounce) cans chopped green
    chiles, drained
1 cup mayonnaise
1 cup sour cream
1 bunch green onions, diced

2 cups sharp Cheddar cheese,
    grated
1/2 teaspoon salt
Cumin to taste
1 to 3 jalapeños peppers, chopped
    and seeded

Combine all ingredients and serve with scoop-size Fritos. It is best to let dip stand in refrigerator for a minimum of 30 minutes before serving. Can be made ahead of time.

Santa Fe Green Chile Dip

Makes 3 cups

1 (10-ounce) can diced tomatoes,
    drained
1 (4-ounce) can sliced black olives
1 (4-ounce) can diced green chiles
3 green onions, chopped, including
    some of the light green parts

2 tablespoons olive oil
1 tablespoon vinegar
1/2 teaspoon garlic salt
Salt and pepper to taste

Combine all the ingredients in a bowl. Chill and serve with tortilla chips.

Southwestern Black Bean Dip

Makes about 2 cups

2 large cloves garlic, minced
1/2 large red bell pepper, chopped
1/2 medium onion, chopped
1 teaspoon vegetable oil
2 (15-ounce) cans black beans,
    rinsed and drained well
3 tablespoons fresh lime juice

1/4 cup fresh cilantro leaves
    (packed), washed well
1 teaspoon ground coriander
1 teaspoon ground cumin or to taste
1/2 teaspoon cayenne
Freshly ground black pepper
1/4 teaspoon salt
2 tablespoons water

In a large, nonstick skillet, cook the garlic, bell pepper and onion in vegetable oil over moderately low heat, stirring until onion is translucent. Remove skillet from heat. In a food processor, pulse black beans, lime juice, cilantro leaves, spices and water 3 to 4 times, adding up to 2 more tablespoons of water, if necessary, to reach desired consistency. Add onion mixture and pulse 2 to 3 times. Chill dip, covered, at least 3 hours and up to 1 day.

Chile Con Queso

Makes 6 cups

2 cups chopped onion

4 cloves garlic, chopped

2 tablespoons olive oil

2 (14-ounce) cans chopped tomatoes, well drained

2 (6-ounce) cans Ortega green chiles

1 cup evaporated milk

2 pounds old English cheese, cut in chunks

Salt to taste

Simmer onions and garlic in olive oil. Add well-drained tomatoes and chiles. Simmer until onions are done. Add milk and cheese. Simmer and stir with patience. Salt to taste. Serve with tostados or Fritos scoops.

Chunky Guacamole

Makes 2 cups

2 large ripe avocados, chopped

2 medium tomatoes, chopped

1 small onion, finely diced

1 (4-ounce) can chopped green chiles

1/4 cup cilantro, coarsely chopped

Juice of 1 lemon

Salt to taste

Chop all the ingredients fine. Do not mash. Mix together with lemon juice and add salt to taste. Serve as a dip or with tostados. May add 1/2 cup diced jalapeños for extra spice.

Roasted Tomatillo Guacamole

Makes 1-1/2 cups

1 or 2 fresh jalapeños, stems removed and chiles halved and seeded

1/2 medium white onion chopped

1 garlic clove, peeled

1 tomatillo, papery skin removed

1 avocado, peeled and cut into chunks

1 tablespoon lime juice

1/3 cup loosely packed cilantro leaves, chopped

1 teaspoon salt

In a large unoiled skillet over medium heat, pan-roast the jalapeños, onion, garlic and tomatillo on all sides, 20 to 25 minutes total. In a blender, whirl the vegetables with 1/4 cup water until blended but still chunky. Add avocado and lime juice: pulse until blended. Add cilantro and salt, pulse to combine, and add more salt and/or lime juice to taste.

Nachos de Lamy

Makes 60 servings

10 corn tortillas
Cooking oil
Refried beans
Jalapeños, thinly sliced

Shredded Cheddar or longhorn
    cheese
Guacamole

Preheat oven to 350 degrees F. Cut the tortillas into sixths and drop in hot oil until they float (or about 30 seconds). Remove and drain off excess oil. On each section, place 1 tablespoon of the refried beans. Next, place a slice or two of jalapeño on top of the beans and then cover with some Cheddar cheese. Place in oven until cheese melts. Top with 1 tablespoon of guacamole and serve immediately.

Josefinas

Makes 24 servings

8 Mexican hard rolls or one loaf
    French bread
1 cup drained canned green chiles
    or fresh chopped green chiles
2 sticks (1/2 pound) butter,
    softened

1 clove garlic, minced
1 cup mayonnaise
8 ounces Monterey
    Jack cheese, grated

Preheat broiler. Slice the rolls crosswise into 1/2-inch slices and arrange on a baking sheet. Toast until bread is golden on one side. Rinse the seeds off the chiles, drain well and chop. Mix with the butter and garlic. Mix mayonnaise and cheese. Spread cheese mixture on untoasted side of the bread slice. Broil until the cheese is brown and puffy. Serve at once.

Chile Cheese Appetizer

Makes 18 servings

1/2 cup butter
10 eggs
1/2 cup flour
1 teaspoon baking powder
Dash salt

1 (12-ounce) can chopped green
    chiles or fresh chopped green
    chiles
1 pint cottage cheese (small curd)
1 pound Monterey Jack cheese

Preheat oven to 325 degrees F. Melt butter in 13 x 9-inch pan. Beat eggs in a bowl, add flour, baking powder and salt; blend. Add melted butter, chiles and cheeses and blend. Bake 35 to 40 minutes. Cut into small squares to serve.

Pâtés and More

Navajo Squaw Dance, 1936, by Stanley Mitchell, Navajo, #51397/13. Museum of Indian Arts and Culture/ Laboratory of Anthropology, Department of Cultural Affairs, www.miaclab.org. Photo by Blair Clark.

Avocado Pâté with Parsley and Pistachios

Makes 8 to 10 servings

Vegetable oil

4 ripe avocados, peeled and pitted

2 (8-ounce) packages cream cheese (room temperature)

2 tablespoons shallots or green onions, minced

1 tablespoon fresh lemon juice

1 teaspoon garlic, minced

1 teaspoon chili powder

1/2 teaspoon salt

1/4 cup fresh parsley, chopped

2 tablespoons unsalted pistachios, chopped

4 leaves butter lettuce or Boston lettuce

1/2 cup pitted black olives

1/2 cup chopped Roma tomato

Tortilla chips

Line a 6-cup rectangular glass loaf pan with 3 layers of waxed paper, extending over long sides only. Brush top sheet of paper with oil. Puree avocados and cream cheese in a food processor. Add shallots, lemon juice, garlic, chili powder and salt. Blend 30 seconds. Transfer mixture to prepared pan; smooth top. Press plastic wrap onto surface of pâté and refrigerate at least 6 hours or overnight. Remove plastic from pâté. Unmold onto rectangular platter. Remove waxed paper. Mix parsley and pistachios in a small bowl. Sprinkle over pâté. Arrange lettuce decoratively at corners of platter. Garnish with olives and tomatoes. Surround with tortilla chips.

Roasted Garlic, Olive and Goat Cheese Pâté

Makes 8 servings

Olive oil

2 large cloves garlic

16 ounces pitted black olives (save a few for garnish)

4 ounces soft goat cheese (e.g., Montrachet)

1 teaspoon black pepper

Parsley for garnish

Preheat oven to 325 degrees F. Cut off the ends of garlic cloves; place on a double layer of foil and drizzle with olive oil. Wrap and seal the foil; place in the oven for about an hour. Remove from oven, open packet and allow garlic to cool slightly. While garlic is baking, drain the olives; place the olives on several layers of paper towels and wrap tightly (try to get rid of as much liquid as possible). Take a few and slice them for garnish. Squeeze the garlic cloves out of their "shell," place cloves in the food processor along with the olives, goat cheese and pepper. Process until the consistency is a uniform paste (pâté); adjust the seasoning (salt and pepper), if necessary (the olives are salty, so you shouldn't need to add much, if any, salt). Store in the refrigerator. Serve at room temperature. Garnish with sliced olives and parsley. Serve with small toasts or crackers.

Mushroom Pâté

Makes 1 to 1-1/2 cups

1/2 small onion
1 clove garlic
1/2 pound mushrooms
1 tablespoon butter
1 teaspoon oregano
1 tablespoon chopped fresh parsley
1 tablespoon chopped chives
1/4 teaspoon salt

1/2 teaspoon freshly
   ground black pepper
10 ounces almonds, toasted
1 tablespoon sherry
1 tablespoon heavy cream
Parsley and pimento
Crackers

Mince onion, garlic and mushrooms together in a food processor. Do not puree. Sauté mixture in melted butter until liquid evaporates. Add herbs, salt and pepper. Process almonds in a food processor fitted with a steel blade until coarsely chopped. Add mushroom mixture, sherry and cream; process until fairly smooth, but with a little texture. Pour into a small mold and refrigerate. Remove from mold and garnish with parsley and pimento. Serve with crackers.

Mushroom-Liver Pâté

Makes about 2-1/2 cups

3 tablespoons olive oil
1 medium onion, finely chopped
1 pound chicken livers, cut into
   small pieces (can also use dove,
   quail or pheasant)
1/2 pound mushrooms, sliced

1/4 cup dry sherry
3 tablespoons parsley, minced
2 garlic cloves, pressed
2 tablespoons soft butter
Salt and freshly ground pepper
Pinch nutmeg

Heat the oil in a large skillet over medium heat. Add onions and sauté 2 to 3 minutes. Add livers and mushrooms and cook until livers are no longer pink. Transfer with a slotted spoon to a blender or food processor in small batches and process to a paste. Add remaining ingredients and seasonings to taste, and mix thoroughly. Chill overnight. Serve with Melba toast or party rye or pumpernickel.

Lobster Pâté

Makes 4 to 8 servings

1 (8-ounce) package cream cheese,
   softened
1/4 cup dry white wine

1/8 teaspoon dill weed
1/2 teaspoon each seasoned salt
   and onion salt
2 cups lobster meat, finely chopped

Beat the cheese and wine until creamy. Add other ingredients and blend. Cover and refrigerate overnight. Serve with crackers.

Bacon and Walnut Pâté Mousse

Makes 8 servings

10 slices bacon, diced
1 pound chicken livers
1/2 cup brandy
3/4 cup heavy cream
1 yellow onion
1/3 cup mayonnaise

1 teaspoon dried thyme
Pinch ground nutmeg
Salt and black pepper to taste
2/3 cup chopped walnuts
4 tablespoons fresh parsley, chopped

The day before serving, fry bacon in a skillet until crisp. Remove and drain on paper towels. Sauté chicken livers in the bacon fat over medium heat until brown, about 5 minutes. They should still be pink on the inside. Remove livers from skillet and set aside. Pour brandy into skillet and stir, loosening brown bits in skillet. Add cream and heat to boiling. Reduce heat and simmer until it is reduced to about 1 cup. Process the livers, onions, and cream in a food processor until smooth. Add the mayonnaise, thyme, nutmeg, salt and pepper. Process until smooth. Add the walnuts, parsley and bacon. Blend into mixture. Put into a serving dish; cover and refrigerate overnight. Serve with crackers.

Smoked Salmon Pâté

Makes about 2 cups

1/2 pound smoked salmon, all bones
    and skin removed
4 ounces cream cheese
1/2 cup unsalted butter

1 tablespoon onion, minced
1 teaspoon cognac
1/2 teaspoon Worcestershire sauce
2 tablespoons fresh lemon juice

Puree all ingredients in a food processor. Transfer to a small bowl and serve with crackers. Keeps, covered in plastic wrap, 3 to 5 days in refrigerator.

Cocktail Pecans

Makes 12 servings

2 tablespoons butter
1/2 teaspoon seasoned salt
1 to 2 dashes Tabasco sauce

1 pound pecan halves
3 tablespoons Worcestershire sauce

Preheat oven to 300 degrees F. Put butter, salt and Tabasco sauce in 12 x 8-inch baking dish. Put dish in the oven to melt butter. Add pecans, stir until coated. Bake 20 minutes, stirring occasionally. Sprinkle with Worcestershire sauce. Stir until coated. Bake until crispy, about 15 minutes.

Orange Pecans

Makes 2 cups

1-1/4 cup sugar
Zest and juice of 1 orange
1/8 teaspoon cream of tartar
2 cups pecan halves

Cook sugar, orange zest and juice, and cream of tartar in a double boiler over medium heat to softball stage. Remove from heat and beat until creamy. Dip pecans into the mixture, forming small clusters, or coating singly if they are large. Keep the mixture in a pan of warm water while dipping. Lay out pecans on a cookie sheet until dry and place them into a serving dish.

Sweet and Spicy Pecans

Makes 3 cups

2 tablespoons unsalted butter
3 cups pecan halves
1/3 cup packed light brown sugar
1 tablespoon ground cumin

1 tablespoon pure chili powder
1 teaspoon paprika
2 tablespoons apple cider vinegar
1/4 teaspoon salt or to taste

Preheat oven to 350 degrees F. Melt butter in a large skillet over medium heat. Add pecans and cook until lightly browned, about 3 minutes. Add brown sugar and cook until lightly caramelized, about 3 minutes. Stir in cumin, chili powder and paprika. Add vinegar and cook until all liquid has evaporated, 1 to 2 minutes. Season with salt. Spread pecans on a baking sheet. Bake until crisp, about 3 to 5 minutes. Cool. Store in an airtight container until ready to serve.

Sweet and Salty Almonds

Makes 3 cups

3-1/2 tablespoons lightly salted butter
1/2 cup sugar
1/8 teaspoon cayenne pepper

3 cups whole blanched almonds
1-1/4 teaspoons regular or coarse salt

In a skillet, melt butter over moderate heat. Add sugar and cayenne pepper. Increase the heat to high and cook for 1 minute, stirring constantly. Add almonds and reduce heat to medium high and cook 6 to 8 minutes, stirring and shaking the pan constantly until almonds are dark brown and pop. Spread almonds on a baking sheet and sprinkle with salt. Toss almonds as they cool. Store in an airtight container until ready to serve.

Navajo Child's or Saddle Blanket, 1900, #09141/12. *Museum of Indian Arts and Culture/Laboratory of Anthropology, Department of Cultural Affairs, www.miaclab.org. Photo by Blair Clark.*

Spiced Pecans

Makes 6 cups

3/4 stick unsalted butter
1-1/2 teaspoons Chinese five-spice
   powder
1/2 teaspoon cayenne pepper

2-1/4 teaspoons crumbled dried
   thyme
1/2 teaspoon salt or to taste
6 cups whole pecan halves

Preheat oven to 375 degrees F. In a large heavy saucepan, melt the butter with the five-spice powder, cayenne pepper, thyme and salt. Stir in all the pecans and toss to coat well. Bake the pecans in batches on cookie sheets for 1 to 15 minutes. Remove from oven and cool. Store in an airtight container.

Lamaze Sauce—A Philadelphia Classic with Seafood

Makes 1 quart

1 pint mayonnaise, chilled
1/2 cup India relish, chilled
1 pint chili sauce, chilled
1 teaspoon chives

1 hard-boiled egg, chopped
Salt and pepper
Horseradish, optional

Mix all ingredients in a chilled bowl. Excellent served with chilled cooked shrimp, lobster or crabmeat.

Sesame Mayonnaise

Makes 3 cups

2-1/2 cups mayonnaise
3 to 4 tablespoons oriental sesame
   oil
2-1/2 tablespoons soy sauce
1 tablespoon rice wine vinegar

1 tablespoon Dijon mustard
1 teaspoon Chinese chile oil
Grated zest of 1 large orange (about
   4 teaspoons)

Mix all ingredients together in a bowl for dipping asparagus or other vegetables.

Peanut Sauce

Makes about 3 cups

1 cup chopped onion
1/4 cup minced garlic
1/3 cup minced fresh ginger
1 teaspoon red pepper flakes
1 to 2 teaspoons peanut or other vegetable oil
6 tablespoons sugar

1/3 cup soy sauce
3 tablespoons cider vinegar
1 cup crunchy peanut butter
1 cup (more or less) coconut milk, unsweetened
1/4 cup cilantro, chopped

Fry onions, garlic, ginger and red pepper flakes gently in oil about 8 to 10 minutes, until onions brown lightly. Add sugar, soy sauce, vinegar and peanut butter to pan. Stir in coconut milk to achieve desired consistency and cook for another 5 minutes, stirring frequently to prevent sticking. Let sauce cool and adjust seasonings. Add more coconut milk, if you like. Stir in chopped cilantro. Serve warm or at room temperature. Keeps a long time. Serve with appetizer-size skewered chicken or beef.

Jezebel Sauce

Makes about 4 cups

1 (18-ounce) jar pineapple preserves
1 (18-ounce) jar apple jelly

2 ounces dry mustard
1 (6-ounce) jar horseradish

Mix all ingredients in a bowl and spread over an 8-ounce block of softened cream cheese with crackers or serve as a side with meat or with a toasted baguette.

Chile Relish

Makes about 1-1/2 cups

1 cup sugar
1 cup vinegar
2 cups fresh green chiles, chopped

1 tablespoon dill seed
1 tablespoon mustard seed

Boil sugar in vinegar until sugar dissolves. Add rest of the ingredients and simmer 30 minutes. Remove from heat, cool and refrigerate. Serve with cream cheese, meats or crackers.

Los Amigos Deviled Eggs

Makes 12 servings

6 hard-boiled eggs
3/4 cup crabmeat, drained and picked (or cooked, chopped shrimp)
2 tablespoons fresh chives, chopped

1 tablespoon mayonnaise
1 tablespoon rice vinegar
1 teaspoon wasabi paste
Salt and pepper to taste
1/4 small avocado
Pickled ginger for garnish

Cut the boiled eggs in half and remove the yolks. Set the whites aside. In a bowl, combine the yolks, crab, chives, mayonnaise, rice vinegar and wasabi. Mix with a fork to blend. Season with salt and pepper. Fork the mixture into each egg half, mounding it. Slice the avocado into 12 pieces and top each egg with a piece. Garnish with a small slice of pickled ginger.

Fresh Peach Chutney

Makes about 4 cups

3 cups peeled fresh peaches
1/2 cup green bell pepper, finely diced
1/2 cup yellow onion, finely minced
1/2 cup fresh red chile pepper, finely diced
1/4 cup apple, finely diced
1/4 cup golden raisins
1 clove garlic, minced

1-1/2 tablespoons ginger, peeled and finely minced
1 cup light brown sugar
3 tablespoons cider vinegar
Salt to taste
Dash of cayenne pepper
Optional: Dash each of cinnamon, allspice and cloves

Place all ingredients in a large saucepan over medium heat and stir well to combine. Reduce to low heat and cook for 30 minutes, stirring occasionally, until chutney begins to thicken slightly. Let cool, pour into container and cover. Refrigerate until ready to serve with cream cheese or bread. Mango may be substituted for peaches.

Parsnip Chips

Makes 6-8 servings

1-1/2 pounds parsnips, peeled
2 quarts peanut oil
Salt

Cut parsnips lengthwise into 1/16-inch-thick slices using a mandolin or a very sharp knife. (Can be prepared 4 hours ahead.) Place in a large bowl and cover with cold water. Drain thoroughly and pat dry before continuing. Heat oil in a deep fryer or large saucepan, to 325 degrees F. Add parsnips in batches (do not crowd) and fry until limp, about 30 seconds. Transfer chips to paper towels, using a slotted spoon. Heat oil to 375 degrees F. Take parsnips in batches and fry until golden brown and crisp, about 2 minutes. Drain on paper towels. Sprinkle with salt and serve.

Mora Deviled Eggs

Makes 20 servings

10 hard-boiled eggs, shelled
2 cloves garlic, finely minced
2 serrano chiles, seeded and minced
1/2 cup mayonnaise
1 teaspoon fresh lemon juice

2 teaspoons dried mustard powder
1/4 teaspoon red chile powder
1/4 teaspoon chopped cilantro
Salt and pepper to taste

Cut the boiled eggs in half and remove the yolks. Set the whites aside. In a bowl, combine the yolks with the remaining ingredients and blend. Fill the egg whites with the mixture and sprinkle tops with chopped chives and paprika.

Cashew Wafers

Makes 75 wafers

1 pound extra-sharp Cheddar cheese, shredded

1 cup unsalted butter, room temperature

1 teaspoon salt

3/4 teaspoon cayenne pepper

1 cup sifted flour

2 cups dry roasted cashews, walnuts or macadamia nuts, finely chopped

Preheat oven to 325 degrees F. Bring cheese to room temperature and beat until smooth. Beat butter, one tablespoon at a time. Add salt and cayenne, and then stir in flour, 2 tablespoons at a time. Add nuts and form into a ball. Chill dough and form into small balls. Place on lightly greased cookie sheets, spaced 1 inch apart. Flatten with a fork. Bake 20 to 25 minutes. Cool and store in an airtight container until ready to serve.

Cheese Straws

Makes about 100 straws

15 ounces extra-sharp Cheddar cheese, grated

1-1/2 sticks margarine

2 cups flour

1-1/4 teaspoons baking powder

1/2 teaspoon salt

6 dashes Tabasco sauce

1 teaspoon cayenne pepper

Preheat oven to 300 degrees F. Bring cheese and margarine to room temperature. Sift flour, add baking powder and salt, and sift again. With hands, mix margarine and cheese well. Add the flour, Tabasco sauce and cayenne and mix well. Place the dough in a cookie press and press onto ungreased baking pans about 1 inch apart. Bake for 10 minutes. Lower the oven to 225 degrees and cook until crisp. If straws are baking too fast, leave oven door ajar. Serve with dips and spreads.

Parmesan Pita Crisps

Makes 8 servings

6 pita rounds

12 tablespoons unsalted butter, melted

1-1/2 cups freshly grated Parmesan cheese

1 cup chopped fresh parsley

Cut around the edge of each pita round, making 2 round halves. Place the rounds smooth side down on a baking sheet. Brush each generously with butter. Cut each round into wedges and cover with cheese and parsley. Broil in oven until golden brown and bubbly. Serve with dips and spreads.

Landscape, *n.d., by Willard Nash, oil on canvas, 24 x 30 inches. Collection of the New Mexico Museum of Art. Photo by Blair Clark.*

Sesame Wafers

Makes 6-8 servings

1 package piecrust mix
1 cup toasted sesame seeds
Coarsely ground salt and pepper

Preheat oven to 400 degrees F. Following package directions, prepare piecrust mix, stirring in the sesame seeds. Roll dough 1/2 inch thick on floured surface, and then cut into small rounds. Put on a baking sheet and bake until golden brown. Remove and sprinkle with salt and pepper. Serve with spreads.

Gorgonzola Wafers

Makes about 30 wafers

1/4 pound (1 stick) butter, room temperature
1/2 pound gorgonzola or other blue cheese, finely crumbled

1 cup unbleached all-purpose flour
3/4 cup pine nuts
1/2 teaspoon salt (optional)

Combine the butter and cheese in a food processor or mixing bowl and blend until creamy. Add flour, pine nuts and salt. Using palms, form into two 1-1/2-inch-diameter cylinders. Wrap each cylinder in waxed paper or plastic wrap and refrigerate until well chilled and firm or overnight.

Preheat oven to 375 degrees F. Slice chilled dough into rounds about 1/8 inch thick and place about 2 inches apart on cold lightly greased baking sheets. Bake until golden brown, about 12 minutes. Immediately remove from baking sheets and cool on wire racks. Store in airtight containers.

Sugared Cheese Biscuits

Makes 50 biscuits

8 ounces sharp Cheddar cheese, shredded
1 cup butter, softened
2 cups plus 2 tablespoons flour

3/4 teaspoon paprika
1/2 teaspoon salt
Confectioners' sugar to taste

Preheat oven to 450 degrees F. Beat the cheese and butter in a mixer bowl until creamy, scraping the bowl occasionally. Add the flour, paprika and salt and mix well. Shape into 1-inch balls. Place on a baking sheet. Bake for 7 minutes. Sprinkle sugar on a sheet of waxed paper. Place the biscuits on the prepared waxed paper; roll in sugar. Serve hot or at room temperature. May be prepared and frozen for future use.

Pistachio Cocktail Bread

Makes 1 loaf

3 large eggs
1/4 cup sugar
1/2 teaspoon salt

1 cup flour
1-1/4 cups shelled, roasted
    pistachios

Preheat oven to 275 degrees F. Line a loaf pan with parchment paper or spray with baking spray. Whisk together eggs, sugar and salt until well blended. Mix flour and nuts together and fold into egg mixture. Do not overmix. Spread batter into pan, pressing into corners. Draw a sharp knife through mixture to help disperse air pockets without too much extra mixing. Bake 45 minutes, until light brown on top. Remove to rack. When cool, remove from pan and wrap loosely in plastic wrap. Place in freezer 1 to 2 hours, or until cool and firm. Slice bread very thinly (1/4 inch or thinner). Slice on the diagonal for larger slices. Place slices on parchment paper on baking sheets (may need 2 pans). Bake 20 to 25 minutes, until golden brown, being careful not to burn. Remove to wire rack to cool. Store in an airtight container. Serve with a wonderful cheese or by itself.

Navajo Women with Corn, *1941, by Mary Ellen, Navajo, #54003/13. Museum of Indian Arts and Culture/Laboratory of Anthropology, Department of Cultural Affairs, www.miaclab.org. Photo by Blair Clark.*

Beve

rages

Nonalcoholic

Horse Race, 1937, by Paul Tsosie, Navajo, #53970/13. Museum of Indian Arts and Culture/Laboratory of Anthropology, Department of Cultural Affairs, www.miaclab.org. Photo by Blair Clark.

Burro Alley Buttermilk

Makes 4 servings

3 cups fresh blueberries
1-1/2 cups buttermilk
1/2 cup sugar

1 teaspoon lemon zest
2 tablespoons fresh lemon juice

In a blender, pulse all ingredients for about
1 minute. Pour into glasses and serve.

Navajo Rug, 1920s, #36994/12. Museum of Indian Arts and Culture/Laboratory of Anthropology, Department of Cultural Affairs, www.miaclab.org. Photo by Blair Clark.

Mint Sparkle Punch

Makes 3 quarts

1 (10-ounce) jar mint or mint-
    flavored apple jelly
1 cup water

1 large can pineapple juice, chilled
1/2 cup lemon juice, chilled
1 (2-liter) bottle chilled ginger ale

Dissolve jelly in water over low heat, then cool. Pour into a small punch bowl or large pitcher and add remaining ingredients that have been chilled.

Patio Punch

Makes 20 (1/2-cup) servings

2 quarts lemonade or limeade
1 quart pineapple juice
1 quart grapefruit juice

2 quarts orange juice
2 quarts chilled ginger ale
Optional: peach or nectarine

In a punch bowl, mix all the ingredients, except for the ginger ale. Add an ice ring made of half water and half orange juice. Add the chilled ginger ale. Optional: float very thin slices of a peach or nectarine for looks and flavor.

Spiced Pineapple Punch

Makes 3 quarts

2/3 cup sugar
1 cup water
3 tablespoons whole cloves
12 whole cinnamon sticks

ADD:
1 large can pineapple juice, chilled
2 cups orange juice, chilled
1/2 cup lemon juice
1 quart ice cubes or frozen
    pineapple juice
1 quart dry soda, chilled
Garnish with frozen fruit slice

Simmer first four ingredients for 15 minutes over low heat. Remove from heat, cover, let cool, and then chill. Strain and pour into a large pitcher or small punch bowl. Add rest of ingredients.

Frozen Tea

Makes 1 gallon

3 lemons

2 oranges

9 family-size tea bags

1 cup chopped fresh mint leaves

3 cups sugar

1/4 cup maraschino cherry juice

Fresh mint for garnish

Maraschino cherries for garnish

Squeeze lemons and oranges. Chill juices and reserve lemon hulls. Boil 2 quarts water, remove from heat, and add tea bags, mint leaves and reserved lemon hulls. Steep 30 minutes. Strain, add sugar and stir until dissolved. Refrigerate up to 24 hours.

When mixture is thoroughly cooled, add lemon, orange and cherry juices, plus 1-1/2 quarts more cold water. Stir well and freeze in 1-gallon ice cream freezer to slushy consistency.

When serving, garnish with fresh mint and maraschino cherry.

Berry Punch

Makes 6 servings

4 peeled, diced (1/4-inch) ripe white or golden peaches

2 cups diced (1/4-inch) ripe cantaloupe

1 cup diced (1/4-inch) ripe strawberries

1/2 cup raspberries

1/4 cup fresh grapefruit juice

1 (24-ounce) bottle sparkling apple cider, chilled

2 teaspoons orange flower water (found in specialty food shops), optional

2 cups sparkling water, chilled

6 mint sprigs, for garnish

Place the fruit in a large glass pitcher. Pour in the grapefruit juice, sparkling cider and orange flower water, if desired. Prefer alcohol? Replace the orange flower water with 2 tablespoons of Grand Marnier or Cointreau. Let rest at room temperature for 1 to 2 hours for the flavors to blend. Before serving, pour in the sparkling water. Serve over ice in stemware or other decorative glasses. Garnish with mint.

Orange Fizz

Makes 1 quart

Juice of 6 fresh oranges

1 cup milk

1/4 cup sugar

3 tablespoons powdered white frosting mix

Put all ingredients in a blender. Add ice and blend until frothy. Serve immediately.

Pueblo Pottery, 1917, by Henry C. Balink, oil on canvas, 27 x 33 inches. Collection of the New Mexico Museum of Art, gift of Mr. and Mrs. F. D. Good. Photo by Blair Clark.

Alcoholic

Acoma Woman Picking Chile, 1936, by Lolita Torivio, Acoma Pueblo, #51446/13. Museum of Indian Arts and Culture/Laboratory of Anthropology, Department of Cultural Affairs, www.miaclab.org. Photo by Blair Clark.

White Sangria with Peaches

Makes 16 cups

2 (25-ounce) bottles dry white wine
(such as white Rioja)

4 cups orange juice

1-1/2 cups Cointreau or other
orange liqueur

2 large ripe peaches, rinsed, halved,
pitted, cut into thin slices

2 lemons, rinsed, cut into very
thin rounds, seeded

2 (11- to 12-ounce) cans
chilled grapefruit soda

Combine wine, orange juice, Cointreau, peach slices and lemon rounds in a large jar. Refrigerate until cold, at least 2 hours. Can be made 1 day ahead; keep refrigerated. Before serving, mix in soda. Serve cold.

Holiday Milk Punch

Makes 8 servings

1 cup sugar

1 cup dark rum

1/2 cup brandy

2 tablespoons vanilla extract

8 cups milk

Optional: nutmeg or cinnamon
for garnish

Dissolve sugar in the rum and brandy in a large pitcher. Add the vanilla and milk, then freeze until cold and slushy. Pour into glasses (add garnish, if desired) and serve.

Campari Cocktail

Makes 1 serving

Ice cubes

1 ounce Campari

1 ounce Punt e mes vermouth

Splash of seltzer or soda water

1/2 slice orange

Fill a 6- to 8-ounce old-fashioned (short) glass with ice, then pour Campari, vermouth and seltzer over ice and stir. Add orange slice.

Photo by Peter Vitale

Fort Marcy Artillery Punch

Serves 100

1-1/2 gallons sparkling apple juice
1/2 gallon rum
1-1/2 quarts gin
1-1/2 quarts brandy
1-1/2 quarts rye whisky
1-1/2 gallons strong tea

2-1/2 pounds brown sugar
1/2 pint Bénédictine D.O.M.
Juice from 1-1/2 dozen oranges
Juice from 1-1/2 dozen lemons
1 bottle maraschino cherries

Make stock with ingredients from 36 to 48 hours before using. Just prior to serving, add 1 case of champagne.

Berry Rum Punch

Makes 8 servings

2/3 cup water
2/3 cup sugar
3 cups fresh raspberries, divided
2 cups fresh orange juice
2 cups pineapple juice
1 cup dark rum

1 cup light rum
1 orange, peeled and diced
1 cup diced, peeled fresh pineapple
1/2 teaspoon vanilla extract
Ice cubes

Bring water and sugar to boil in a medium saucepan, stirring until sugar dissolves. Remove from heat; cool syrup completely. Puree 2 cups raspberries in a food processor. Pour puree through fine strainer set over saucepan with syrup. Press on solids to extract as much liquid as possible; discard solids. Mix orange juice, next 6 ingredients, 1 cup raspberries and raspberry syrup in a glass bowl. Cover; chill at least 4 hours and up to 1 day. Strain into a pitcher. Serve punch over ice.

Mandarin Cocktail

Makes 1 serving

1 ounce Midori liqueur
1 ounce Absolut mandarin vodka
Splash of sour mix

Ice
1 maraschino cherry

Combine all ingredients except cherry in a mixing glass and stir. Pour the mixture into a chilled martini glass, straining out the ice. Drop in the cherry and serve.

White Cosmopolitan

Makes 1 serving

2 ounces citrus vodka

4 ounces white cranberry juice

1 ounce fresh lime juice

1 ounce sugar water

Shake ingredients with ice. Strain into a martini glass. Garnish with an edible orchid, if desired.

Kir Royales

Makes 6

3 tablespoons cassis

1 bottle good champagne

6 twists lemon

Fill the bottom of 6 champagne glasses with 1/2 tablespoon cassis. Pop open a bottle of champagne and divide among the glasses. The color of the drink should be a sunset pink. Garnish with lemon twists.

Blackberry Limeade

Makes 12 servings

2 cups fresh lime juice
   (from 8 to 12 limes)

1-2/3 cups superfine granulated sugar

1 bottle champagne

2 tablespoons blackberry syrup

Thin lime slices

Stir together all ingredients in a pitcher until sugar is dissolved. Serve over ice and garnish with lime slices. Cook's note: To make blackberry syrup, heat 1/4 cup blackberry jam with 1 tablespoon water in a small saucepan over moderately low heat, stirring, until jam is dissolved. Pour mixture through a fine-mesh sieve into a small bowl, pressing on and then discarding solids. Syrup keeps, covered and chilled, 1 week.

Champagne Cocktail

Makes 1 serving

1/2 ounce gin

1/2 ounce Alizé (passion-
   fruit liqueur)

3 ounces chilled dry champagne

Garnish: raspberries

In a champagne flute, combine gin and liqueur and top off with champagne. Garnish drink with berries.

Chocolate Martini

Makes 4 servings

1/3 cup chocolate liqueur
1/3 cup dark cream cocoa
2/3 cup half-and-half

1/4 cup vodka
Crushed ice cubes

Stir together first 4 ingredients. Fill half of cocktail shaker with ice. Add half of liqueur mixture, cover with lid and shake 8 to 10 seconds, until thoroughly chilled. Strain into chilled martini glasses. Repeat with remaining mixture. Serve immediately.

Lemon Martini

Makes 1 serving

1-1/2 ounces Absolut citron vodka
1/4 ounce Triple Sec
1/4 ounce sweet and sour

Combine ingredients with ice in a tall glass or shaker. Shake and strain into a martini glass that has been rimmed with sugar. Fresh-squeezed lemon or lemonade may be substituted for the sweet and sour.

Dirty Martini

Makes 1 serving

1-1/2 ounces Bombay Sapphire gin
or Grey Goose vodka
1-3/4 ounces extra dry vermouth

1 teaspoon olive juice
(or more to taste)
Stuffed green olives

Combine all ingredients except for the olives in a shaker with some ice. Shake and strain into a martini glass and add a stuffed olive for garnish. Stuffed olives for martinis may be separated from the juice and marinated in vermouth or vodka for a while before serving.

Sunset in Santa Fe Martini

Makes 1 serving

1-1/2 ounces orange vodka
1/4 ounce Cointreau
Orange slice

Combine ingredients except orange slice with ice in a tall glass and shake. Strain into a martini glass and garnish with the orange slice.

Tequila Martini

Makes 1 serving

2 ounces Patrón tequila
1 ounce fresh lime juice
Lemon twist

Combine ingredients except for the lemon twist in a tall glass and shake. Strain into a martini glass and garnish with the twist.

Berry Martini

Makes 1 serving

2 ounces Bombay gin
1/2 ounce cranberry juice
Cherry or raspberry for garnish

2 ounces Absolut vodka
1/2 ounce Chambord
Lemon twist for garnish

Combine ingredients with ice in a tall glass and shake. Strain into a martini glass and add garnish.

Canyon Road Martini

Makes 1 serving

1-1/2 ounces Ketel One vodka
2 ounces sour apple pucker
Apple slice for garnish

Combine ingredients with ice in a tall glass and shake. Strain into a martini glass and add garnish.

White Sangria

Makes 4 servings

1 vanilla bean
1/4 cup white grape juice
1 ounce Tuaca
2 tablespoons orange juice
1 ounce brandy

1 tablespoon of sugar
1 bottle chilled sparkling wine
1/2 cup sliced strawberries
12 fresh mint leaves

Mix first 6 ingredients in a pitcher until sugar dissolves. Mix in sparkling wine, berries and mint. Fill glasses with ice. Ladle sangria over ice and serve.

Mulled Wine

Makes about 16 servings

4 bottles Pinot Noir
4 cinnamon sticks
1 orange, studded with about 20
    whole cloves, then quartered and
    seeded

1/2 cup sugar
Garnish: orange slices, cinnamon
    sticks

Mix all ingredients in a large pot (or slow cooker) over low heat. Simmer gently at least 30 minutes before serving (start it about 45 minutes before guests arrive.) Do not boil; it spoils. Wine may be further sweetened with extra sugar, if desired. Serve in wine glasses or clear teacups with additional orange slices and cinnamon sticks.

Mojitos

Makes 1 serving

1 heaping tablespoon sugar
8 to 10 mint leaves
2 or 3 lime wedges
Crushed ice

1-1/2 ounces light rum
Club soda
Sprig of mint for garnish

Combine sugar, mint leaves and lime wedges in your cocktail glass. Mash with a wooden spoon. Fill glass with crushed ice and add rum. Add club soda and stir gently. Garnish with the sprig of mint. You may add fruit to the garnish, if you wish.

Museum Hill Tequila Sour

Makes 8 to 10 servings

2 (12-ounce) cans frozen lemonade
2 cups tequila
2 cans water

1 cup crushed ice
Grenadine syrup
Strawberries or pineapple for garnish

Mix first four ingredients in a blender. Pour into cocktail glasses and add a dash of grenadine syrup. Garnish with a fresh strawberry or pineapple.

Santa Fe Lemonade

Makes 4 to 6 servings

2 cups fresh lemon juice
1 cup sparkling water
3/4 cup sugar
1/2 cup bourbon

1/2 cup vodka
Ice cubes
Mint sprigs for garnish
Dash grenadine syrup for glasses

Combine lemon juice, sparkling water, sugar, bourbon and vodka in a pitcher and stir until sugar is dissolved. Chill. Pour over ice-filled glasses and add mint sprigs and a dash of grenadine.

Mexican Coffee

Makes 4 to 6 servings

4 cups hot chocolate

2 cups dark roast, hot coffee

1/2 cup rum

1/4 cup Grand Marnier

1 teaspoon cinnamon

1/4 teaspoon nutmeg

1 teaspoon vanilla

1/2 cup sweetened whipped cream

In a saucepan, heat the chocolate, coffee, rum and Grand Marnier together. Add the cinnamon, nutmeg and vanilla. Remove from heat. At this point, the whipped cream can be folded into the mixture or the mixture can be poured into cups with a dollop of whipped cream placed on top of each serving. If desired, garnish with sprinkling of ground cinnamon.

Chocolate Eggnog

Makes 4 quarts

3 quarts eggnog, chilled

1-1/4 cups chocolate syrup

1/4 cup rum, optional

1-1/2 cups whipping cream

3 tablespoons sugar

1 tablespoon cocoa

1/4 square (1 ounce) semisweet
chocolate, grated for garnish

In a large punch bowl, combine eggnog, chocolate syrup and rum. In a mixing bowl, whip cream, sugar and cocoa until stiff. Spoon the cream into the eggnog and sprinkle with chocolate garnish.

Optional: add 1 quart chilled dry soda, 1 quart chocolate ice cream and plain whipped cream to the punch. Top off with a few maraschino cherries with stems for sparkle.

Sunset Cider

Makes 8 to 12 servings

2 quarts apple cider or
pure apple juice

3 to 4 cinnamon sticks

1 teaspoon whole cloves

1 teaspoon ground nutmeg

1 (6 ounce) can frozen lemonade con-
centrate plus 1 can water

Juice of 2 oranges

1/2 cup rum, optional

Combine all ingredients in a large saucepan and heat for 5 to 10 minutes over medium heat. Remove spices and serve immediately.

Deer and Fawn, 1936, by Gerald Nailor #53922/13. Museum of Indian Arts and Culture/Laboratory of Anthropology, Department of Cultural Affairs, www.miaclab.org. Photo by Blair Clark.

Sunset Slush

Makes 3 quarts

12 ounces frozen orange juice

12 ounces frozen lemonade

7 cups water with 1 cup sugar dissolved in it

2 cups vodka (whisky optional)

7-up to taste

Mix all ingredients and put into the freezer. When ready to serve, spoon into glasses and add 7-Up. Stir and serve.

Jalapeño Vodka Limeade

Makes 1 serving

2 ounces Absolut vodka

1/2 ounce fresh-squeezed lime juice

3 very thin jalapeño slices

Lime wedge for garnish

Pour vodka and lime juice into a tall glass with ice. Shake and strain into a martini glass. Add the jalapeño slices and lime wedge.

Banana Daiquiris

Makes 4 servings

1-1/2 bananas, peeled and sliced

3 ounces crème de banana

1/2 cup white rum

2 ounces simple syrup

1 ounce orange juice

3 ounces half-and-half

2 ounces sweet and sour (can use 2 tablespoons fresh lime juice)

1 to 2 cups ice

Pineapple wedges or maraschino cherries for garnish

Put all ingredients in a blender and blend until smooth. Pour into glasses and garnish, if desired.

Champagne Fizz

Makes 1 serving

1 sugar cube

2 teaspoons apple brandy

1/2 ounce cranberry juice

4 ounces brut champagne

1 apple slice for garnish

Drop the sugar cube into the champagne flute. Add the brandy and cranberry juice. Very slowly pour in the champagne and gently stir. Try not to disturb the sugar cube. Place the apple slice on the rim of the flute and serve.

Sangrita

Makes 6 servings

8 ounces tomato juice

2 jalapeños, seeded and chopped

2 ounces lime juice

1 teaspoon Worcestershire sauce

4 to 6 dashes Tabasco sauce

Salt and pepper to taste

2 cloves garlic, chopped

1/2 teaspoon prepared horseradish

Ice

Shot of tequila per person

Combine all ingredients except for tequila. Blend and pour into glasses. Serve with a shot of tequila.

Mimosa

Makes 4 servings

2-1/2 cups orange juice

2 cups chilled champagne

Orange segments and/or mint springs for garnish

Pour orange juice in champagne flutes halfway and top off with the champagne. Garnish and serve.

Winter White Liqueur

Makes 1 serving

1 ounce Stoli vanilla vodka

1/2 ounce Godiva white chocolate liqueur

1/2 ounce peppermint schnapps

Ice

1 maraschino cherry or mint sprig for garnish

Combine all ingredients in tall glass and stir. Strain into a chilled martini glass and garnish with a cherry and/or mint sprig.

Interior Courtyard of Pueblo, Santa Clara, New Mexico, ca. 1883, oil on canvas, 65-3/8 x 48-7/8 inches. Collection of the New Mexico Museum of Art, gift of Mr. and Mrs. John A. Hill in memory of Maurice N. Mikesell, 1975. Photo by Blair Clark.

Cookbook Committee

Chairman
Dorothy Black

Vice Chairman
Dixie Burch

Gena McKee

Compiling Consultants

Joan Black	Harlene Geer
Katsey York	Colleen Harris

Recipe and Food Consultants

Susan Buddendorf	Alicia Kitzman
Lois Chiarto	Ron Peterson
Pat Eitzen	Francine Pevow
Carolyn Hummer	Judy Womack

Museum of New Mexico Foundation Project Advisor
John Stafford

Contributors

Ida Allen	Stanford Cox, Jr.	*Kathryn Huelster	Sharon Parcel
Mary Atkinson	Jeanne Craig	Carolyn Hummer	Ron Peterson
Janie Bacchus	Joanne Craig	Linda Humphries	Francine Pevow
Thomas Bailey	Patty Dakhli	John Ireland	Nancy Pierce
Cheri Berry	Mimi Doherty	Cindy Johns	Dana Pratt
Lillian Bidal	Rosalind Doherty	Colleen Kistner	Helen Pynn
Dorothy Black	Cindy Dunham	Alicia Kitzman	Nina Rangel
Joan Black	Pat Eitzen	Matty Kyle	Jane Robb
Stephanie Black	Linda Eppes	Lynne Loshbaugh	Carolyn Sedberry
Sally Blair	Carol Farwell	Kay McFall	Ruthie Sumner
Bonnie Blough	Beth Forester	Gena McKee	Sally Traub
Jerry Brown	Jamie Gagan	Dottie Miller	Mary Wade
Suzanne Brown	Julie Gamble	Marjorie Morehead	Ellen Walton
Susan Buddendorf	Nancy Moore Gehman	Nora Naranjo Morse	Judy Womack
Dixie Burch	Harlene Geer	Renata Mutis	Sharon Wright
Lois Chiarito	Ginger Grossetete	Randy Myers	Liz Werthem
Joan Chodosh	Colleen Harris	Susanna Orzech	

Index

Navajo Rug, 1920-1940, #45292/12. *Museum of Indian Arts and Culture/Laboratory of Anthropology, Department of Cultural Affairs, www.miaclab.org. Photo by Blair Clark.*

Picking Cactus Fruit, 1936, Wilson Dewey, Apache Western San Carlos, #51358/13. Museum of Indian Arts and Culture/Laboratory of Anthropology, Department of Cultural Affairs, www.miaclab.org. Photo by Blair Clark.

Metric Conversion Chart

Liquid and Dry Measures

U.S.	Canadian	Australian
¼ teaspoon	1 mL	1 ml
½ teaspoon	2 mL	2 ml
1 teaspoon	5 mL	5 ml
1 tablespoon	15 mL	20 ml
¼ cup	50 mL	60 ml
⅓ cup	75 mL	80 ml
½ cup	125 mL	125 ml
⅔ cup	150 mL	170 ml
¾ cup	175 mL	190 ml
1 cup	250 mL	250 ml
1 quart	1 liter	1 litre

Temperature Conversion Chart

Fahrenheit	Celsius
250	120
275	140
300	150
325	160
350	180
375	190
400	200
425	220
450	230
475	240
500	260